JUMP
WITHOUT A
PARACHUTE

CASEY —
STAY TRUE TO YOU!
KEEP JUMPING!
♡ CORY

Gall

- ASH

STAY TRUE TO YOU!
KEEP SHINING!

JUMP WITHOUT A PARACHUTE

How to Find the *GUTS* to Leave
the Job You Hate for One You Love

CORY CALVIN

ISBN: 978-1-7339306-3-5 (paperback)
ISBN: 978-1-7339306-4-2 (ebook)

IMPORTANT DISCLAIMER

This publication contains materials designed to assist readers in evaluating their personal careers for education purposes. While the author has made every attempt to verify that the information provided in this book is correct and up to date, the author assumes no responsibility for any error, inaccuracy, or omission. Some names and identifying details have been changed.

www.jumpwithoutaparachute.com

For orders or inquiries, please use the website.

Cover Design by 100Covers.com
Interior Design by FormattedBooks.com

THE FREE

JUMP
WITHOUT A
PARACHUTE
COMPANION
COURSE

To help guide you through *Jump Without A Parachute*, I created a free *Companion Course* that you access, which includes downloadable worksheets, bonus video content, and lists of resources and links mentioned in this book. This is your first step toward success with the content of this book, so I highly recommend you sign up now. The supplemental materials in this free course are organized by the sections and chapters of this book, making it easy for you to find what you need as you read along.

There's also a bonus section with content beyond what is shared here in the book, including interviews to help you on your journey. I'll be adding more material to this bonus section over time, so make sure to visit the web address below and get free instant access to it now! See you on the inside!

Visit the following link to get free access to your *Jump Without A Parachute* bonus materials now:

DEDICATION

To my second-grade teacher,
Miss Joyce Miller

CONTENTS

INTRODUCTION

MY "SUCCESSFUL," AWFUL, TYPICAL CORPORATE LIFE

I used to work for the Fortune 50 company PepsiCo at their World Headquarters in White Plains, New York. I was super successful. It was terrible.

I vividly remember Sunday evenings as a corporate executive. After shopping at Whole Foods, I would make the trek to my $3,600-per-month, 800-square-foot one-bedroom apartment. Once there, I unloaded my food for the week into the refrigerator and kitchen area before kicking off my shoes. Then I would walk into the living area to rest for a few moments before meal-prepping for the week, dreading the five days ahead of me and wondering where the weekend went.

My gut began to churn, thinking about what Monday would bring. A dreaded early rise to my alarm on my phone followed by a normal routine of preparing for my workday in a stuffy corporate environment. Putting on clothing that certainly looked nice but felt like a prison uniform. Codes of conduct. Rules. Boredom. "Success."

I would trudge downstairs and get into my eight-year-old, 2009 Pontiac G6, waiting for me among all of the BMWs, Audis, Mercedes, and Range Rovers belonging to the others in my building, a constant reminder that while I was certainly doing well, I was never doing *well enough*. While my lifestyle afforded me a comfortable living on the Upper West Side, my surroundings did an incredible job constantly reminding me of all I still hadn't achieved.

As I drove into work Monday morning, my body stiffened and my nerves jolted, resisting what I was about to do. I often enjoyed taking the longer route to work, because it helped me avoid the office for a little longer. It was my way of not having to think about my day ahead for just a few more moments.

I would think, *it shouldn't feel like this.*

My stomach clenched as my inner voice began to wonder if I was truly happy. Was this my dream job? Was I living my best life every day? Was I following my passion? I was successful, and I should have been enjoying that success—but instead, every fiber in my body was telling me to quit.

It took too long for me to realize I had surrendered my time, my happiness, and my soul to a system that I (and you) learned from society. Go to school, get a job that pays the bills, and save money for retirement—a system that unconsciously controlled my life. I thought this was the only way, completely unaware that there may be another system—another path.

"Is this the only life for me?" I would ask myself, walking up the cemented sidewalk that meandered to one of the building's side entrances. The building was beautiful, but I hated every moment I was inside it.

What if I quit? That would feel so amazing. I would be free and could travel. I wouldn't feel like I was held hostage anymore.

But, my inner voice—a product of that system— argued, *in one more year, I can get promoted to a Senior Director.* My annual bonus would go up to 30% of my salary, and I would begin earning stock options that vest in three years as part of the executive compensation platform. I'd be earning well over a quarter of a million dollars a year. I could move into the global marketing department, representing brands like Pepsi and Mountain Dew. *Yes, that is what I want to do.*

But did I want this because I actually wanted it, or because I had been coached to think about my trajectory with the company as the only basis for determining success in life? Could I even find success outside the corporate ladder?

I had made it to this in-group. I was worthy. I brought a different perspective from my unique finance and consulting background. Furthermore, I *chose* to be here. I wasn't forced to be here. It was my decision, one I made six years prior. I wanted to work for a large, global company that viewed diversity and inclusion as a major platform of their company's culture so I could come out and be myself in my workplace. I knew this company would allow me to learn new skill sets and obtain new positions every two to three years. I could advance within the company and not feel bored or stuck in one position for many years.

Only one problem: I felt bored and stuck anyway.

I chose all of this. But why would I continue to choose to be a part of a group that gave me anxiety? I not only felt the constant pressure of deadlines, but also the pressure of performing at a high level. It seemed everyone around me thrived on the pressure. I'm not sure they really thrived, but if they were faking it, they certainly could get an Oscar for their performance.

I even remember the line item in my job description: "Must be willing to work under pressure." My ego would never let me say no to that, especially when I had convinced myself that this is my optimal path.

Turns out, my method of working well under pressure was closing in on myself every time I faced it. It became normal to walk into meetings with senior executives and even junior employees feeling like I was a fish out of water. My eyes nervously darted at the clock on the wall praying for the meeting to end, hoping I wouldn't have to speak up, at the risk of sounding unintelligent.

As my tenure within the corporate world advanced, it felt like I was being pulled through a process against my will, like a stubborn dog trying to sit down as it is being pulled on a leash. All for what? Was I truly making a difference in someone's life? Was I making the world a better place? Or was I just existing as a cog in the corporate machine to earn a paycheck to support a comfortable lifestyle?

Something inside of me was not quite right. I had this burning desire to live my life on my terms. Not on the terms of a company. I wanted to be free. I wanted to be able to control my life every day, not only the weekend. I wanted freedom to walk my own path, but it was strange to think of a different path. It felt scary and full of unknowns. Why would anyone with a well-paying job and great benefits leave that?

I was working on cool brands that most people know around the world. There was prestige in that. The company was moving toward healthier products with natural ingredients, which was something I was passionate about. I had been promoted several times over the past six years and moved up the corporate ladder very quickly, each step bringing a multitude of benefits.

All these accolades, corporate advancement, and bonuses pushed me to want to work harder and see how far I could go. I had intentionally made every decision that got me to this point, but my gut was still screaming,

"Get out of here." I was successful, but I was inexplicably unhappy, and this dissonance drove me crazy. With each passing day, repeating the same tiring routine with nothing but time off work to look forward to, it began to occur to me that I had bought into an awful system that had complete control over me.

THE SYSTEM

This system tells us that when we graduate high school, we should go to college if we want to earn a higher-paying job. And after we graduate from college, we need to find a job with benefits in our field that doesn't feel like work and at the same time earn enough to afford to live on our own.

They make it sound so easy. So easy, in fact, that if you don't or can't do it for one reason or another, you feel like a failure.

So, we do it. We join the corporate system and learn another specific path. We are rewarded in many ways to keep us working. We need to work for 35 years to pay our bills and save enough to retire, they tell us. Then when that moment comes, you hold a party, serving cake and cocktails with current and former colleagues who tell funny stories about the time you walked into the women's room at work or the time when the CEO was so angry that you almost got fired. All these memories can be relieved in a three-hour party. We run out of stories before the party's over. And finally, once the party ends, we have time to relax and do the things we want to do.

Ahh, but wait, now we are 65 years old (or older), and all those things you dreamed of doing at this age are now thought of in a different way. Your body has changed, your patience level has adjusted, your ideas have shifted. Maybe you wanted to travel the world when you were 40 and your body was fit enough to do so, but at 65, the idea of going scuba diving seems too far out of reach. We have the money and the time we diligently saved up, but we can't use it.

That's the path we're told to get on, or face failure.

By the way, a retirement party can be the perfect ending to a happy, fulfilling career for some people. But my guess is that if you picked up this book, you don't want that path.

I was doing everything I was taught. I had a great job with an incredible title—Director of Corporate Strategy—where many of my peers were impressed with my resume. The company valued me as a human being and accepted all of me. The people I worked with were extremely intelligent and I was challenged every day by them. I saved for retirement, had great health benefits and made enough to live a convenient lifestyle. I lived in New York City, a place where most people dream of living and working. I was advancing and could get promoted even further. I had a life many people dream of. I had the life *I* used to dream of.

Why would I give any of that up?

I was beginning to see the system, and was beginning to ask: Is this what I signed up for? Is this the path I have chosen? But while I felt the need to ask the question, I couldn't find a satisfactory answer. Truth is, I didn't know of any other path. That was the trajectory I'd known my entire life and my entire career. I received an undergraduate degree and a graduate degree in business. I had become a corporate executive and built a prestigious career. So while I had anxious feelings in my gut questioning my choices, I quelled those feelings because I was on the path that I learned, the only path I could take to success and happiness—though, why it hadn't actually *led* to happiness, I wasn't sure.

For a second, I thought "what if?" What if I left and tried something new?

WHAT IF?

For a while, I researched paths that seemed different, but were still corporate. I looked online at other positions in New York City. It all sounded so glamorous. Job titles with fancy job descriptions and all of the buzzwords. Opportunity for advancement. Competitive executive salary with bonus compensation. Progressive work environment. Blah blah blah. I could see behind their facade, now. All the descriptions really said the same thing: "Work. Follow the corporate breadcrumbs. Make money. Retire with less money than you'd like. Be too old to enjoy your freedom." I realized that this was the same path I was already on, so it wasn't worth the risk to leave what I had only to jump to something that was pretty much identical.

I needed something new, but what became so apparent after the "what if?" repeated in my head was that this was the only path I was taught. My head spun even more.

I would have to make up a whole new path if I wanted to escape the one I was on.

I thought about how I could create my own new path, a path I was passionate about—but one I could work on while still employed. While this new passion ramped up, I would have a safety net. Then, once it was ready, I could leave the corporate world and begin walking this new, fulfilling path full time.

THE CATCH

In short, my attempt to create a new path while still following my old path didn't work.

As someone who had always searched for the perfect, badass wallet, I thought I discovered a potential consumer niche and business opportunity. I hired a freelance designer in India to create a unique, slim wallet design, reached out to low-cost, overseas manufacturers, attempted to set up a simple supply chain for the wallets to reach the U.S. customer, created an online marketing strategy primarily utilizing social media, and planned to sit back and watch revenue grow. Until I realized how multiple time zones and my lack of time to dedicate toward building and selling a product from scratch quickly impeded my mental momentum.

I quickly learned that 24 hours in a day is not enough. Many of us work for eight to nine hours a day and commute for around one hour, sometimes more. Our bodies require us to spend time eating food and sleeping. This eat/sleep combo takes up eight to ten hours. This leaves about four hours of free time. However, remember, we need to get ready in the morning. That is another hour. And if we want to stay healthy, we must exercise, so that is another hour or so. No wonder we feel so drained.

That's the catch: when you work full time, you have very little time to do anything else. Many people argue that you have weekends, you can sleep less, you can carve out time during lunch, etc. Sure, you can find a little bit of extra time here and there, and sure, you can use that time to work on building a new opportunity for yourself. That is, if you are single, don't have children or a close family, and don't want to hang out with your friends. This method works in a very controlled environment, which is true of less than one percent of the population.

You can quickly see why the idea of creating a new path while working a full-time job is nearly impossible. A full-time employee has very little time to concurrently build another business. I certainly don't want to deter anyone and say that it isn't possible to pull off, but it is very difficult. Creating the initial wallet prototype proved to be too much of a hurdle to manage, and as my energy levels fizzled, so did my dream.

For me, what worked was going all in. Jumping without a parachute was the only way for me to find this new path and follow my passion.

JUMPING WITHOUT A PARACHUTE

The principles in this book are based on my experiences and the lessons I had to learn in order to make my new path. This book is for the person sitting in their cubicle day in and day out, looking out the window, wishing there was a more fulfilling way to live and earn. This book is for the person who says "one day" they will travel the world (or fill in the blank to a passion of yours), but at the moment they are too busy with their nine-to-five. This book is for the person who says "I don't like what I am doing now, but I don't know what I want to do with the rest of my life." It's for the person who says "I can't afford to live my passion and dreams. I need to work to survive."

This book will help anyone struggling to realize there is a way out. It's not always easy, but the journey is your reward. Life will be better as a result.

Since I left corporate America in November 2017, I have created a transformational travel company leading retreats that help individuals overcome their fears and harmful mental patterns and begin living the life of their dreams. Along the way, I have also written a bestselling memoir, spoken to corporate groups like LinkedIn about my transformation, and traveled to all seven continents and over 60 countries. I have the flexibility to live and work anywhere I choose and am on track to earn more income than I ever did as an executive.

Now on Sunday nights, I go to bed excited for the week ahead. On Monday mornings, I wake up without an alarm around 8am instead of being jolted out of bed at a heart-wrenching 6am. While the world is in rush-hour traffic, I am at home, working out and getting my blood flowing. I use my creative energy to write text for future books and online courses, record interviews with inspirational people for my podcast, research adventurous destinations around the world, plan unique, life-changing retreats, and coach interesting and driven clients toward ultimate life success. I create my own schedule each day!

I created all of this on my own. I have failed over and over, but through these failures, I have learned so much more than I ever learned in the corporate world. I've discovered the meaning of my life and my higher purpose. The corporate world allowed me to remain comfortable, but I had to get uncomfortable to begin living.

My corporate skills have provided a great foundation, but now I'm vested. In a corporation, other team members typically handle tasks unrelated to your function. I've had to push myself each day to learn something new and figure things out on my own (like finding my writing voice while writing, editing marketing videos, finding my target audience, executing marketing campaigns, managing negative feedback, etc.).

During my corporate career, my role was limited to a specific job description, my advancement was predicated on prior "resume" experience and my earning upside was capped based on my job level within the corporate hierarchy. But now my upside is endless, and ultimately up to me. I'm no longer just a worker with a badge and an employee ID number. I am in control of my own destiny.

I am truly living the life of my dreams. I am living proof that there is a path out there for you. You can have it all. You can do what you love AND you can have a healthy income to support your lifestyle WHILE saving for retirement AND enjoying health benefits.

Just like anything in life, this will take some work. If you aren't willing to work hard and make a commitment to yourself, or if you aren't brave enough to jump without a parachute to find a more fulfilling path, then this book isn't going to help you. You have to be ready to act. You have to be ready to make a change in your life.

Stop dreading Monday morning. Stop giving in to the corporate machine that keeps you chained to the system. Begin failing. Begin living. Begin chasing real success and real happiness.

Go on. Jump.

HOW TO USE THIS BOOK

This book is broken out into three sections. First, in Part 1, I will tell you how I made my jump. Part 2 walks you through the five lessons I learned to help teach you how to jump. Finally, in Part 3, it will be your turn to jump.

While you read, you will notice at the end of each chapter (with the exceptions of Chapters 9 and 10) a reference to the online *Companion Course* to this book. I've created this free course where you can download worksheets and templates that will allow you to solidify the thoughts written in this book and apply them to your own life. I've also included some bonus content for you to help guide you even further along the way. To get free access to the *Companion Course*, which I recommend you use while you read this book, go to:

www.jumpwithoutaparachute.com/course

Get ready to jump.

PART 1: MY LIFE

WHEN I GROW UP

SECOND-GRADE ADULTING

My second-grade teacher, Miss Miller, with her tall figure and broad shoulders, stood at the front of our class curiously asking us, "What do you want to be when you grow up?" It was the proverbial question that would be asked throughout our schooling and probably something I have asked myself at least once a month since the second grade. Miss Miller stood looking around the room through her thick glasses wondering who would be bold enough to speak up first.

"I want to be a football player," one of my classmates shouted proudly. Other kids began to speak out about occupations we all saw frequently: teachers, firefighters, police officers, veterinarians.

No one ever said insurance agent, data analyst, strategy consultant, assembly line worker.

Think about all of the careers the people around you have, and the percentage of those who are professional athletes, firefighters, police officers, veterinarians. Many of us know teachers, so this is an exception, but generally the percentage of people living those childhood-dream careers is very low.

Yet, we all grow up to be something.

Of course the object of this question asked at such an early age isn't to have the student nail down their future career, but it is an exercise in having young minds think about life after school. The teacher is helping the student see themselves not sitting in a classroom, but "adulting"—somehow.

In the second grade, I hadn't given life after graduation much thought. My only concerns were lunch, recess, and what I would be doing after school that afternoon. I had no desire to be a professional athlete, because someone told me that the odds of being an athlete were super small. I had no interest in becoming an electrician like my dad because he came home dirty every day from work and I didn't like getting dirty. I didn't want to be a teacher like my mom was studying to become because at the time, I had neither heard of nor seen a male teacher (times have certainly changed). Nor did I want to become a farmer like my mother's parents, nor drive a beer truck like my father's father did.

As I sat in the small wooden chair in the middle of the airy classroom, I thought back through all of the fun I had over the summer, trying to figure out how that might translate into a mysterious, "grown-up" job. I loved building mazes in the sandbox for my pet guinea pig. I spent hours inside of my playhouse creating mazes out of old TV trays. I even created the first dead animal museum in Montpelier, Ohio, collecting specimens I found around my quiet neighborhood.

I was constantly thinking of creative things to do outside. My curiosity came naturally. But it was hard to line up "curiosity" with a career.

"Cory, what about you? What do you want to be when you grow up?"

How would I explain to Miss Miller what I was thinking about? Everyone else in the class knew what they wanted to be right away.

"Well, I am not sure what the word is," I quietly said with an unsure tone. "But I love to create things. And I'm curious about how things are made. I want to create new things that don't exist yet."

"So you want to be an inventor!" Miss Miller responded. A smile came to my face since the word sounded fancy. Yes, that's it! An inventor. I reveled in the fact that no one else thought of this. I was unique. I stood alone.

I could see myself sitting in front of a large blank piece of paper on a flat table in the middle of a clean workshop, like a lab. I would draw out solutions to problems, like a modern-day Thomas Edison. I envisioned solutions that helped others live a more enhanced and fulfilled life, which made me happy and proud of my contribution to society.

MAJOR IN INVENTION

As I progressed through school, the same question kept appearing. "What do you want to be when you grow up?" It was a constant barrage to help us think about our future. However, as I continued to answer this question the same way, I had an overwhelming feeling that being an inventor was stupid. No one else wanted to be that. In fact, when I read through all of the books about careers, there was no career title of "inventor."

During our eighth grade English class, we were asked to write about the question and share with our peers. I stood up in front of the class. The professional athlete wannabe glared at me as if he was going to beat the snot out of me on the playground after lunch. My high-pitched voice trembled while I read: "I want to use my creative mind to become an inventor. I want to invent new things that haven't been created yet that will help others live a happier life."

With such relief that my turn was over, I walked back to my desk in the middle of the room and I could hear the jock snicker and whisper, "No one becomes an inventor, faggot."

He then stood up and detailed his life as a professional football player, surrounded with money and mansions. I was beginning to see society's priorities. (By the way, that "pro football player"? He ended up bouncing from job to job because he couldn't pass a drug test wondering how life got away from him.)

Once I entered high school, I became less sure of my career goals. Maybe inventors only lived back in the early 1900s, when they created everything that was to be created, like electricity and automobiles. Maybe my career aspirations were as far-fetched as being a professional athlete.

Beyond mazes for my guinea pigs, I tried inventing a few things that I imagined might be useful, like embedding a chip in a wallet to unlock doors at your home and electronics that didn't need to run with batteries or cords. I also created a lot of fun things like haunted houses for the neighborhood kids in my playhouse and a pretend amusement park in our backyard using various contraptions from trees. I dreamed of building an actual roller coaster in our backyard.

As my brain learned new cognitive paths and I continued fighting for social acceptance, doubt began to dispel some of my earliest passions.

As children, we are encouraged to dream without limits. To believe that we can be whoever we want, that we can do whatever we want. That being the President of the United States is not a far-fetched idea. That walking on Mars one day is not a matter of if, but a matter of when.

But as our brains are exposed to our surrounding environment and then molded by the mental choices we make as a result, limits form. Barriers and obstacles arise.

At one point, I truly did want to be a full-time inventor. Creation took me to a happy place. But society crept into my mind to say I should not pursue this. There was no major in invention at college. It wasn't "realistic." What would my father think?

Impacted by my external environment, my peers, and my family's opinion, the pragmatic part of me thought that I would never make any money to support myself as an inventor. While I would love creating new things, I knew I would eventually need something else to fall back on. I told myself that being the next Thomas Edison was only a dream, and I had to choose a "real job." Before long, I had convinced myself that my creative career choice was not an option for me.

How many times do we go through this thought pattern in life? What is the intersection of pursuing dreams and earning enough to support our daily life? Is money a deterrent to following our dreams, which then becomes a deterrent from true happiness? We hear all of the time that we should find something we love to do each day and it won't feel like work. But then we also hear that we need a job to earn money to support our life. Then, even if we find something we truly love to do, but it doesn't support our life—or maybe we just *think* it won't support our life—we reject it and go for the safer option. The corporate fallback.

After my reality check, I thought about "realistic" options: I could go into a specific trade, like being an electrician like my father. I could go into the military to get my schooling paid for and travel the world (all while exploring my sexuality? No—it was bad enough being closeted in a small town, never mind being out in the military). I could go to college and major in something. Or I could just get a job out of high school and not do anything else.

None of those really excited me.

CAREER DAY

On career day during my sophomore year, I was asked the question again. They reminded us we'd have to pick very soon—as if we didn't know that yet. When I said I simply didn't know what I wanted to do when I grew up, I was told to think back about things I loved as a child.

I remembered the guinea pig mazes, but pushed them out of my mind, telling myself again that being an inventor was impractical and off the table. Then I remembered riding in the passenger seat of my father's truck at the age of ten and feeling my eyes almost pop out of my head as the skyline appeared in the distance. We emerged through the Chicago Sky Way bridge that led into the city and I fell in love, instantly, with the buildings' tall, sleek facades. I knew I had to walk among the masterpieces created for function and living.

I decided to put two things that I loved together: creating and skyscrapers. And that is what I would become, a world-renowned architect designing incredible structures for others to use, observe, and enjoy.

The guidance counselor seemed satisfied, and nobody gave me funny looks anymore when I said what I wanted to be when I grew up. I decided that this was it. I had successfully chosen the career I would have for the rest of my life.

"Architect" seemed like a good answer to that "what do you want to do when you grow up" question, but looking back, I wish that someone would have asked me why. If only someone asked me: Why do you want to be an architect? What do you love about creating? How do you feel about creating buildings every day?

I thought my experience in Chicago was unique and special and was a sign of my destiny to be an architect, but isn't everyone wowed by an incredible skyline? If it were that simple to become the things we love, we would have millions of architects. And that jock would be a professional football player.

Looking back, I've come to understand there is a much more complicated path when it comes to deciding your career.

At 18 years old, all I wanted was to finish school and graduate, thinking how awesome it will be to leave home and be on my own, finally. Answering deep questions about my future was far from my mind. I knew I would need to focus on a career one day, but I had my whole life ahead of me for that. Now that I had the goal of "architect" in mind, I figured I would just take the path on my way to that goal as it came.

If I really would have spent time diving into answering questions about why I chose my ultimate college major, I believe I would have chosen a completely different career. Instead, it took a lot longer for me to figure that out and find an "ultimate career."

CAREER PATH

After finally deciding I wanted to be an architect, I was thrilled to have been admitted into a prestigious architecture program at Ball State University.

I looked up at the intimidating, dark-brick building that housed the College of Architecture, thinking how this is the beginning of the rest of my life. Someday, I would be *making* buildings just like this one, I thought to myself. For some reason, that thought didn't bring back the breathlessness of the Chicago skyline. In fact, I didn't feel excited about that thought very much at all.

Eager to begin the first class of college, I sat down in the front row of the large hall that contained over one hundred students because I arrived minutes before class was beginning.

As the dean welcomed us to the beginning of our college careers and congratulated us for making it into such a prestigious program, my stomach began to shift, the type of uncomfortable feeling you get when something isn't quite right. When your body communicates with you to say you are out of place.

The same feeling I got every Sunday night of my corporate career—but I'm getting ahead of myself.

Replaying every step I took to decide on a future career and a college major that led me to select this out-of-state school (Ohio had many excellent and qualified schools to attend), it seemed logical to try to ignore my body's natural response. I figured it was just nerves from taking a first big step into the unknown so I just tried to pay attention to the images of historic buildings flashing up on the large screen directly in front of me.

I breathed in the stale air of the theater-like learning environment as my skin moistened. I took some notes, but the rest of the class was a blur. I felt completely out of place. But why?

"It's your first day of college. Give yourself a break," I told myself, realizing that I was experiencing great change with my life. I wasn't about to toss my whole career path out the window just because I had first-day jitters. However, the doubt wouldn't leave my mind.

Two days later, after I reluctantly forced myself to go back to the introductory class, the internal pressure intensified. I didn't understand why I was feeling this way. I *belonged* here. I grew up engineering mazes in my sandbox for my guinea pig. I spent high school taking mechanical drawing classes. I had built a portfolio of creative projects in high school art class to gain admittance into a prestigious architecture program. This is what I was supposed to be when I grew up.

I suddenly realized that none of my preparation mattered anymore. I didn't belong here.

Ten minutes into the second class, I stood up out of the creaking seat, pulled my backpack up over my shoulder, trying not to cause a disturbance and hoping the professor wouldn't notice, walked up the aisleway of stairs dividing the seats and exited out the door at the top of the stairway. After walking a few blocks, I knocked on my counselor's door, in desperate need of someone to speak with.

How could this happen? I sat in front of my counselor defeated. All of those genius moments of creativity from my childhood felt rendered obsolete. I had practiced for the "what do you want to be when you grow up?" question for most of my life and I lost all of it in a matter of a few days.

"Well, what other things have you considered?" my thirty-something counselor calmly inquired from across her small desk. Here we go again with: "What do you want to do when you grow up?" This question wouldn't go away—but the secret was that it never had to. If I would have known this question would replay itself over and over for nearly the next twenty years of my life, I would have found more peace in that moment. I didn't have to decide on the answer once and for all—but it sure felt like I did.

I flashed back to Miss Miller asking me the same thing. I felt just as lost as I did then. Isn't there a better way to know the answer to this question than pulling it out of thin air? And what if I didn't ever figure out the right answer? I didn't have a backup plan. I was now attending an out-of-state school as a result of a singular fact: its prestigious architecture program. Changing paths felt like the biggest deal in the world—and unlearning that idea took a lot of work further on down the line, work I wasn't ready for yet.

We played a round of "process of elimination," eliminating everything that didn't sound interesting to me. There were so many specialized fields to go into, but nothing really stood out to me. I had no interest in the medical field. I had no interest in political science or communications. Any creative field like architecture required admittance to a program, and at that point in time I had not yet built any experience to be admitted, so that felt impossible.

I was embarrassed and felt that everyone else had it all figured out. I graduated second in my high school class, but wasn't smart enough to have an inkling of what I would do for the rest of my life. I felt that I was at a crossroads that most people come across much later in their career, even those kids who seemed certain in their eight-year-old desire to be a firefighter.

"I've always loved playing the game Monopoly. I love dealing with money," I recalled thinking aloud during that conversation with my career counselor. To this day, I have never lost a game of Monopoly. Everyone in my family stopped playing with me because I always won. Maybe that was my calling, not the Chicago skyline, not the guinea pig mazes.

It wasn't as simple as "liking Monopoly," but after a process of elimination combined with an exercise on interests, my career counselor directed me toward business.

During the first day of the Introduction to Business class, the professor said something that I remember vividly to this day. "You will have at least seven career changes throughout your career." When you hear bold statements like this, it is common to doubt the prediction. My eyes rolled back a little as my mouth scrunched. I was already on number two and I hadn't even made it through a year of college yet. I didn't intend to change five more times. I was sticking with this career forever. I was going to follow the corporate path and do it "right." I was *not* going to go through the hell of changing the direction of my career ever again.

I'm currently on career number nine.

It is incredible to think back at how many times in my life I had to make a decision about my future. It still continues to this day. The only difference? I still don't always know the answer, but the question doesn't scare me anymore.

The lesson that has stuck from my Introduction to Business course was not the *number* of careers we will have in our lifetime, but the fact that when we pick one, it doesn't have to remain the only one we pick. I wish someone would have told me to find something interesting RIGHT NOW, instead of trying to make me wire my brain into believing that my decision was FOREVER.

In fact, everyone wants to do many things. Of course it is difficult to pick just one.

Has something like this ever happened to you? You invest time, energy and money into a path that seems so right for you, but when it comes time to implement your "strategy," it feels wrong. You feel trapped. Suddenly every part of your being rejects this new path you have created, but when looking back at all you had invested into getting here, you feel sick at the thought of starting over with something new.

It took a long time for me to stop feeling sick at the thought of changing careers, but eventually the lesson stuck that my career doesn't have to be forever—and neither does yours.

When I looked back at my young life and realized all of my hobbies and play time didn't necessarily add up to one single career path, I used to feel like a failure for wasting the time, I should have used to find out my "one true path." Now I know that my varied interests are a benefit. My hobbies and playtime show how huge the runway of my future really was. Not having one single goal actually meant I had more freedom than I ever thought possible.

So if you also don't know what you want to be when you "grow up" (even if you're already grown up!), don't worry. It's a good thing.

Now it's your turn:
- ❏ Think about what you want to be when you grow up (as a child and now)
  - ❏ What happened to your dreams as a child?
  - ❏ Are you pursuing this path now?

ONLINE EXERCISE

Go to "Chapter 1 - When I Grow Up" of the *Jump Without A Parachute Companion Course* at **JUMPWITHOUTAPARACHUTE.COM/COURSE** for your first exercise, which will take you back to the very beginning to better understand the building blocks of your career journey.

PRODUCT OF YOUR ENVIRONMENT

LEARNING THE PATH

Have you ever wondered who you would be today if you had different parents or caregivers growing up?

Well, stop thinking about that because you can't change it. It's hard sometimes to admit (especially as you get older) how much your life has been influenced by your caregivers. It's more than we might wish. How you think, how you act (or react), how you manage conflict (or don't manage conflict), what is important to you (and not important to you), your thoughts about being on time, your views about relationships, your overall outlook on life—these were all influenced by our caregivers, and the list goes on and on. So many things are learned from the environment and the people you were surrounded by at an early age.

While these are not specific lessons outlined in a life workbook, these are things you learned from observing and experiencing firsthand. You watched your mother clean the house so you learned that it is a good idea to clean the house. You watched your parents argue over something (or maybe you didn't see your parents argue at all) and you learned how to manage yourself in an argument (or maybe you learned that conflict is not good). And as a result, you learned how to forgive and love unconditionally (or maybe you did not).

You observe all these lessons, but how are you able to know what is normal and what is not? What is right and what is wrong? It's almost like it creates a fallacy. We trust our parents, so we therefore trust their behaviors are normal and the right way.

I'd like to think I only pulled the best traits from my mother and father, but I know I have characteristics influenced by them that I am not so proud of. We can't pick and choose which traits we are exposed to and which traits we end up adopting; however, we can choose how we manage those characteristics in our adult lives. But this is only IF we recognize those characteristics we want to adjust. We'd first have to realize the thing we learned isn't so good. But how would we know, if that is all we learned? For many, they don't understand what it would be like to do the opposite of what it is they learned.

Just like the wannabe football player turned perpetually unemployed. His parents lived paycheck to paycheck, hating their blue-collar factory jobs. After work their hard-earned income purchased alcohol and other substances to help them forget about the day of work. Their mental and emotional abuse, lack of love, and attitudes toward work and income was what the football player inadvertently learned. And, through learning, he eventually became his parents.

As a young kid, I remember my father sharing with me many times that he dreamed of owning his own business. He had so many ideas, like creating his own body shop, building and selling small-scale trains that you could ride on, creating a woodworking business for household cabinetry, buying the local Ace Hardware shop, creating his own electrical business, and buying real estate and becoming a property manager.

It was exciting to listen to my father talk about owning his own business. Words like freedom and financial independence and business owner sounded so cool. He dreamed of being his own boss and not making money for someone else. He dreamed of having the freedom to work on projects that excited him instead of working on projects that were just a means to earn money.

While my father often shared his dreams of being a business owner, all that ever became of the dreams was that: just nice dreams. Thoughts of "what if" and "one day" and "maybe when I retire" kept him from manifesting those dreams into reality. As a child, I could never quite figure out what held my father back. And now, at the same age as my father was when he shared his dreams with me, I can see how comfortable it is to dream but never take action.

I learned from my father that dreaming is natural. We all have hopes and dreams of doing something "one day." But I also learned from my father that it was easier to stay employed and on the path you are on. You can have your dreams, but it doesn't usually "make sense" to follow them.

Similarly, while my mother took care of my sister and me for most of our childhood, she had always yearned to become an educator. Once my sister and I went to preschool, she began attending a nearby college to earn her degree in education. I remember one winter day that heavy snow resulted in our school closing, so my mother took my sister and me to class with her.

We went to the college bookstore to pick out some fun notebooks to draw on during my mother's zoology class. The desks were unlike anything I had seen in my kindergarten classroom and each row of desks was tiered, sloping down toward the professor at the front of the room. I looked around seeing people much older than me listen intently to the professor and was impressed that even grown-ups can endure school just like me. I thought I was pretty cool being a college kid for the day.

My mother worked hard. Looking back, I'm still not sure how she was able to go to school full time while taking care of my sister and me before and after school. When did she have time to study?

When I saw my mother standing among the other graduates a couple years later in her long black gown and fun black hat, I was proud. She pursued her passion during a very time-limited moment in her life. Sacrificing many things, she went after what she wanted. She could have easily said "I will do what I want to do 'one day'" but she instead realized that the present moment was the right time.

I've always admired my mother for going after her dreams, among many other things. She knew what she wanted and she went for it. My mother eventually became a second-grade teacher at the same school that my sister and I attended when I entered the third grade.

I watched. I listened. I learned from each of my parents.

My parents approached "following their dreams" in very different ways—namely, my mother followed her dream, while my father didn't. Regardless, they both followed a similar path in their career: they found a job that benefited them at the time and they stuck with it. While my father worked for several different companies, his profession and role didn't change much, despite his dreams of creating his own business. While my mother changed grade levels and took on additional roles now and then, she stayed at the same school as a teacher. Consistency in career, whether you followed your dream or not, was the only way to go about it in my family.

I learned from my parents that there is one path for everybody. The correct path was to find something you liked to do and follow it without faltering. This path also meant working for a company or organization as an employee. You study and work hard to learn a craft, and then you find a position that fits within this new learned craft. You continue to work hard and work through adversity as it pops up. If you don't like your working environment or position, then find a similar position that is better, as my mother did when she changed grade levels. And follow this path until you retire later in life. If it's risky to follow your dreams, like my dad thought it was to follow his, don't bother. Discuss it on wistful nights, but don't throw away what you have on a risk.

DEAD END

At each step of the way as we grew up, a collective group of influencers—teachers, parents, older siblings, celebrities, stories through media—helped, educated, guided, and molded us. But then what? Once we reach a certain point of adulthood and we are settled into the current phase of our life, this incubation period has come to an end. Who is now going to help, guide, and mold us?

The obvious answer is this: you are going to guide yourself. You now get to live your life on your own. While this is mostly liberating, it is also very scary to be an adult, all on your own. Make decisions on your own. Earn your own income. Meet other people on your own. Build relationships on your own. Plan your own future.

What do you do when you are suddenly without a guide? You follow the familiar path that you have watched those older influencers follow your whole life. You follow the path that you subconsciously learned along the way. You might feel like you are free, but you are tracing their footsteps without even realizing you're doing it.

It's like a GPS system: you punch in the destination (in this case you punch in your "life goal") and the map takes you to where you want to go automatically, turn by turn. You rarely zoom out on the full map to see the whole landscape. You just trust the GPS system because it has been programmed by very smart people to take you to where you need to go (on autopilot). Similarly, you automatically trust your brain that has been programmed (through a series of millions of moments) to get you to where you need to go.

Most of the time, your GPS takes you to your destination in the fastest way. The journey went as planned and you move on with what you need to do at your destination, taking on a new journey. You never had to think about the decisions that allowed you to arrive.

But have you ever experienced a moment where you had an inkling that the GPS was wrong? Has your GPS system ever taken you down a path that turned out to be a dead end? Or down a route that is not paved or not ideal to take? Did you end up following it anyway, even getting lost because you put too much trust in the GPS? Since you were in autopilot mode, you made the decision to go where the GPS led you, regardless of your instincts.

What do we do when we run into a dead end and feel stuck in life? When we feel trapped?

The interesting part is that our brains have been trained to stay the course and to continue along this path (on autopilot). While we are able to solve smaller dilemmas we face (like when will I find time to clean my house or what will I do during the weekend), our brains haven't had the training to handle more complex issues like the following:

- My life hasn't gone how I hoped and I feel stuck. So how do I get out of it?
- I've lost confidence in myself and no longer know who I am
- I had expectations of my life at this point like being married with children (or remaining happily married) but that has not happened the way I expected
- I trained for a long time for this career, or I have this high-paying job, but I am not happy

Herein lies the issue: You arrive at what feels like a dead-end situation and your brain tries to push forward, but it doesn't know how. That is not how it was programmed. That is not what you learned from your influencers. Our brains have been taught one way. We feel we need to stay on this path and the thought of jumping to a new path seems way out of the question. If this path isn't working for us, *we* must be the problem.

Our mind says stay on the path and figure a way through the obstacle. But our gut is telling us to change course. What happens when you realize that the path you were taught is not the path for you?

You realize that there is more than just one path.

I felt I had to follow the path of my father and mother. It took a big dead end—realizing I dreaded most of the days of my life—to make me jump off that path and into the unknown.

I followed the corporate path on autopilot for years before I found the courage to listen to my gut, shut off the GPS, and trust my *own* sense of direction.

Now it's your turn:

- ❑ Think about what areas of your life have been influenced by your upbringing.
  - ❑ Have these influences been helpful toward your success?
  - ❑ What areas would you want to change?

ONLINE EXERCISE

Go to "Chapter 2 - Product Of Your Environment" of the *Jump Without A Parachute Companion Course* at **JUMPWITHOUTAPARACHUTE.COM/COURSE** and complete the exercise designed to help you understand how you became the person you are today.

I WANT TO BE RICH

*"Choose a job you love and you will never
have to work a day in your life."*

*"Find something you love to do each day
and you will be rich."*

How many times have we heard statements similar to these?

I think most of us realize the meaning behind these
statements and we are smart enough to know they are true.
They are statements I have heard throughout my life, over
and over, from my parents and from other influencers.

After I was directed into the business world in college and entered the white-collar workforce, I worked my way up corporate ladders quite successfully. I got my health benefits, my yearly raise, my nice apartment, my two weeks of vacation time a year. I got the kind of money that signified success to me, my parents, and society. Yet, as I looked out the window of my corporate cubicle, this statement often popped into my mind: Why was I spending most of my life doing a job that I didn't love?

The truth is inspiring, but the reality was sobering. Maybe I loved my job "enough" to endure the days when I wasn't truly happy. Maybe I only "loved" my job for the benefits, the money, and the prestige. But the statement at the beginning of this chapter doesn't say, "Find something that you love to do 'enough' each day and you will be rich." The statement infers we will jump "all in" to that "something," whatever endeavor that may be.

Now sure, no endeavor is 100% perfect. Many tasks within this endeavor require you to endure something that you aren't "in love" with. However, the difference is that when you find something you truly love doing, the remedial tasks or the unloved tasks that are required become tolerable. The remedial tasks are something you will gladly do because you know it is helping you do something you love. But when you begin procrastinating every task, they become a red flag that you aren't in love with what you are doing.

When I procrastinated even waking up in the morning because everything in my job felt like a slog, I was practically living in a world of red flags. It just took a long time for me to address them.

This idea of how doing what you love means never "working" also feels like a "dreamer" statement to many. A statement that may seem impossible to achieve. We are taught implicitly that only a few people have this kind of life. During these moments of looking out the window of my tenth-floor cubicle, this statement seemed so far out of reach for me. It seemed impossible to truly find something that I loved to do every day, because I didn't know what I wanted to do.

I wanted to create things, help people, make mazes for guinea pigs, travel the world. None of that could make me the money I needed, so I felt I had to stay in my corporate job. The job would give me the money to do these things as hobbies—while sucking away all the time I could have to even *do* any hobbies. I found myself in the dead end of a maze, where the only way out was backward. And who wants to go backward?

And then I started making these statements and hearing similar statements from others.

This isn't my dream job, but it pays well
I'm just doing this job to save up
enough money to leave one day

*This job has amazing benefits so I stay
even though I'm not happy*

*I wish I could follow my passion, but...I
have to put two kids through college
I have a mortgage to pay
I have bills to pay*

*I wish I could do that but I don't have any money
I dream of traveling the world but I can't afford it*

*When I retire, I will have enough money
and time to do what I want to do*

I call these "surrender statements." A statement you say to others and to yourself that you are surrendering your current happiness as a sacrifice to eventually get what you want. It becomes a way to rationalize to yourself that this path is okay. You are saying that while you are not 100% happy, you are still a decent percentage happy, and that is good enough. You let these statements bar your windows and keep you in your job, despite your unhappiness.

My mother loved being an educator, but my father was an electrician because he enjoyed it...to a certain extent. He enjoyed building and problem-solving. However, being an electrician was not his main passion.

He had so many other passions that he wished he could pursue. But the money and the benefits were so great as an electrician that he stayed. He endured.

My dad dreamed. He wished. But he stayed because of money. He could see another path, but was too afraid of failure, so he lived a life of mediocrity. And I, a product of my environment, was on track to do the same.

I remember my parents talking about saving money for things they wanted to do, like buy a new car or a nice camper, but never following through, only repeating those surrender statements.

We are a product of our environment. We learn our viewpoint about money from, guess who: our caregivers.

My parents taught me a good work ethic, but being in the closet drove me to want money and status beyond what they had to prove myself. I learned to make money, to be able to have the things I wanted, because I wanted to be seen as successful, not just as gay. I had a burning desire to be known as who I was, not as the person I was assumed to be, in that small town, because of my sexuality. I had a push to show that I had a lot of money, because that, I believed, was how you measured success.

So while I knew money was just a means to live the life you wanted, I associated money with success early on in life. Money was how I could be as successful as my parents. Money was how I could get people to see me for who I am, and respect me. And money, more than personal success, meant happiness. The ultimate life to have. To earn enough money to then have everything you want.

I stared out my office window and sighed. I had money, I had success, but I still wasn't happy. I needed a change. A big change.

I needed to jump without a parachute.

Now it's your turn:
- ❑ Have you ever used a "surrender" statement to rationalize your happiness? If so, which one and why?
- ❑ What ratio of your job is enjoyable vs. not enjoyable? Are you ok with this ratio?

ONLINE EXERCISE

Go to "Chapter 3 - I Want To Be Rich" of the *Jump Without A Parachute Companion Course* at **JUMPWITHOUTAPARACHUTE.COM/COURSE** for an exercise to dive deeper into money and your career.

PART 2: HOW TO JUMP

LESSON 1:
LISTEN TO YOUR GUT

YOUR BRAIN, YOUR HEART, YOUR GUT

Did you know that the gut is lined with a network of millions of nerve cells? These cells are connected to the subconscious part of your brain. So when you have a gut feeling, your brain is the one sending signals to your tummy.

I've heard the phrase "gut feeling" many times throughout my life. In many tough situations where I have had to make some sort of decision, I've always said to myself, "Listen to your gut," in an attempt to help find the best possible outcome.

But at times, I have found it very difficult to make sense of it all. Because, let's be honest, does listening to your gut really work?

When a situation full of many details and difficulties arises, we rarely pay attention to everything that is going on in the body. The brain is wired to use its stored intelligence and past experiences for survival. You have created these mental pathways over time through the influences of situations and of other people. The brain wants to logically think through the decision and use your stored intelligence to produce the correct answer. We want to know for sure that this is the best answer for now.

The heart is your feeler. Your compassion and empathy are stored in your heart. It is where all the soft feelings are produced when faced with a tough decision. We typically want the best, but we don't want to create incremental discomfort for ourselves. The heart protects you from getting hurt.

Of course both the mind and the heart are important. In tough situations, your brain may be saying no and the heart may be saying yes, or vice versa.

But what is your gut doing? Connected to your subconscious brain, your gut produces intuition without the influences of all the patterned brain experiences that often hold us back. The gut bypasses the heart, the protector. The gut is your raw decision-maker.

I know when tough situations come up for me, it is extremely hard to decipher between my heart, my mind, and my gut. I can feel my gut saying one thing, but then my heart or my mind chimes in and says something else. And it feels like I am spinning around in circles. Anxiety builds and my entire body gets worked up. I have felt completely helpless at times, like all I want to do is just not make any decision because it is too overwhelming.

SIMPLE VS. COMPLEX

Simple decisions are fairly easy and quick to make. Do I want to go to the gym tonight? Do I want my triple venti latte with no foam today?

And then there are decisions that are not as easy to make but can be made easily with a little thought. Where do I want to go on vacation this year? Which neighborhood do I want to live in? I've been dating someone for a couple months but it isn't going that well, what do I do?

Then there are the huge, complex situations in our lives that are not that easy to manage. These situations often have many interconnecting parts like a car engine. They typically all flow together, but when something goes wrong, it is very difficult to diagnose the exact problem. So we must peel away the layers.

Complex situations can often look like this…

- I'm unhappy with my career or job but I don't know what I want to do or how I will make money. What do I do?
- I feel stuck in life. I'm not where I wanted to be at this age, but I have no idea how to get my life back on track. What do I do?

I've experienced both of these at once. My gut was screaming so loudly: leave your unhealthy relationship, leave your job, leave your career, travel the world, and figure out your higher purpose in life. Find out what you truly want.

My gut screamed at me for years, but my mind and heart were holding me back. To leave my relationship, I would have to do the hardest thing I've ever had to do in my life. I would have to confront my partner and tell him that this no longer would work. It was something I had done before, but we always seemed to get back together. Him standing in front of me dejected was the hardest thing to see. But I knew I had to do it, and not give in this time.

Now for the second problem: how often I caught myself staring out the windows of the corporate office wishing I wasn't there. My mind certainly had a stronghold on my thoughts of leaving the corporate world. Here is how it would play out:

I wish I weren't here right now. I like my job, but it isn't fulfilling. I should start looking for another job. Wait, wouldn't I just be following the same path that I have followed: another corporate job that seems good for a year or two but then puts me right back here, looking out a window wishing for another job or company?

Why don't you just leave your career? You daydream all the time about traveling and going to remote corners of the globe. Just go do it now. It sounds like the most incredible dream.

Well ok, but if I left my career, how would I make money? What about my health benefits? How would I save for retirement? And I've worked my entire career to get to this point. I'm an executive with a Fortune 50 company. I'm working in corporate strategy, something people greatly desire to do but have to put in so many hours to reach this point. Here I am creating presentations for the Board of Directors and CEO. This is a dream come true.

And give up the money I'm earning? I am living such a comfortable life. I live in a one-bedroom apartment in a building with a doorman who opens the door every time I arrive. I'm right on the Upper West Side, a block from Central Park and a couple blocks from Lincoln Center. I have a car in Manhattan and a dedicated, covered parking space. Who has that? Who *leaves* that?

BUT WAIT

I had no idea what to do outside of this corporate path I had been following. How would I create something that mattered to me and would pay my bills? I wouldn't be able to live in a city like New York because I wouldn't be able to afford it.

All of my education was in finance. All of my job experience was in finance. I invested a great amount of time and money to reach this level of my career. Sunk cost fallacy had unknowingly overtaken my brain. Sunk costs are things like money, time, and effort that have already been spent and cannot be recovered, so you feel you must continue the endeavor as a result. I felt that I couldn't just leave now and start over with something else because of all that I had already invested in the path I was on.

On top of not feeling that I could just leave my money, time, and effort behind, my brain created the story that I could double down and keep climbing the corporate ladder. I could earn more, be seen as even more successful than I already was, and have more of everything I wanted.

But wait. I was still not happy. But wait. I didn't know what else I would do.

If I left my company now, I would need to pay back my relocation fees. So I was stuck for two more years. And if I left then, I'd lose all of the unvested stock options and bonuses that would be coming my way. So I could stay longer to earn those. I can do anything for two more years, right?

BUT WAIT....

This thought pattern happened almost weekly for years. It was a constant barrage of mental chatter. My mind would quickly rationalize all of my unhappiness and repackage it as "even though you are unhappy, it is the least risky path to just stay where you are."

My gut would churn. Each Sunday evening. Each Monday morning commute. Each meeting with my super-smart boss or super-smart colleagues. I had so much to offer and it was illogical to leave, but I didn't want to be there. My gut kept screaming for me to get out, and I kept ignoring it.

WAITING FOR SOMETHING BAD TO HAPPEN

Isn't it interesting that even though we know there is a high probability that we will be happier if we do what our gut tells us to do, we still don't do it?

The pain has to be strong enough. Something horrible has to happen for us to make the tough decision and do what our gut says to do.

What I have seen in my experience is that people only listen to their gut when they are forced to. How many times do we see others begin to follow their happiness in life when there is a death in the family? Or when they lose their job? Or when they have a serious health issue or get into a bad accident?

When something tragic happens, we realize life is way too short to be living a life with partial or even full unhappiness. It forces us to reevaluate our lives to that point. We make different choices and follow a different path. It becomes a forced rewiring of your brain to stop procrastinating what you know you need to do. What your gut has been telling you to do all along.

I began writing this book slightly before the beginning of the coronavirus pandemic hit the United States, and I finished the book when everything had shut down and we were required to shelter in place.

This pandemic is a great example of something happening to us that we never expected. Yet it did happen, and it infused fear and uncertainty into our minds. All of the things we once could do, we could no longer do in an instant, without any mental preparation.

When something tragic and unexpected happens, use it as your moment. Make it the turning point in your life and finally listen to your gut. You may never have a moment like this in the future that provides this much life pause to take action. What are you waiting for?

For me, the pressure built up for so many years until one day I just wanted it bad enough. I stopped using my brain and the mental patterns that held me back for so long and finally listened to my gut.

Your gut is one of the most powerful tools built into your body. We often have complex situations arise that require us to take action. Even not doing something is an action. Our brain, heart and gut all are providing input based on the situation and previous learnings, sometimes providing conflicting input. Pause and listen. While it may be difficult to manage all of the input at the same time, your gut knows the truth. Listen to your gut and then take action.

Now it's your turn:

- ❏ Write down the moments you listened to your gut in life.
  - ❏ What happened then?
  - ❏ Did it work out for you?
- ❏ What does your gut tell you now?
  - ❏ If you aren't doing what your gut tells you to do, why not?

ONLINE EXERCISE

Go to "Chapter 4 - Lesson 1: Listen To Your Gut"

of the *Jump Without A Parachute Companion Course*

at **JUMPWITHOUTAPARACHUTE.COM/COURSE**

and get ready to listen to your gut!

LESSON 2:
WRITE YOUR
2-COLUMN RESUME

THE RESUME WRITER

As we progressed along this path of life, the path of go to school, get a job, make money and retire, our lives began to focus heavily on our career. We were taught at an early age to create a resume: a one- to two-page document to showcase what we have to offer a prospective employer. We write down our objective and summary of qualifications. We list out our job titles and the years we were employed at various organizations. We describe our accomplishments to show other employers how we could also help them achieve their goals. We are taught that this is important, that it lies between us and that dream job. Yet most of us hate writing them.

I was the odd duck. I loved writing resumes; I was creating a masterpiece. I was proud of my accomplishments and it was a challenge to organize all of the data in a neat, black-and-white structure. I liked deciding which data points needed to be included to amplify my chances of being noticed.

This sales tool was a beautiful piece of art for me, a representation of how well I was following the path of life. As the years of my executive career progressed, my resume grew to two pages and it was tough to fit all of my experiences into this brief document. My entire life's work neatly summarized on two pieces of paper showcasing my strengths.

And for those in a more creative field, a portfolio was created to give someone a sense of the capabilities that make up your professional career. With a resume and/or a portfolio, we spend a lot of time summarizing our life.

Yet apparently, our whole life—or, everything important in our lives, anyway—can be squeezed onto a page or two.

But are the words on your resume or the pieces in your portfolio everything that makes up who you are? Since high school or college, we have written down everything we know about ourselves onto this simple document, but while it is meant to be an introduction to us and our lives, it is actually missing a lot.

I love to think of an image of an iceberg when it comes to thinking about our full lives. Envision the small white area of an iceberg bobbing up and down above the water. However, what the human eye does not see is the much larger portion of the iceberg below the surface. The part below the surface is usually more than ten times the size of the portion above the surface of the water.

RUNNING AWAY

When I eventually built up the courage and confidence to no longer trade unhappiness for money (I will share how I did this a little later), I left the corporate world behind without having any idea what I would do with the rest of my life.

Then I began to think about this concept of the resume. This is the external portion of your life that everyone can see, the part that, through the hours of high school and college and every time anyone asked what we wanted to be when we grew up, seemed to be the most important. But what about the 90% of your life that no one can see on a resume? The portion under the surface. *That* is where our true happiness lies.

And it struck me: what if we added a second column to our resume? The left column would remain the same: full of our job titles, companies, and achievements. However, the right column would be all of the unseen. The intangibles would be listed, like feelings, emotions, fears, and reactions. It would marry your resume with your diary.

One day while on vacation, I decided to pull out my resume and I began writing my right-hand column. I wrote down what I enjoyed about the position, what I did not enjoy, my favorite memory, and what was occurring in my life at that time. Then I gave it an overall grade (A, B, C, D, F).

And something fascinating occurred. My "life's DNA" appeared right in front of me. It was like a life sequence code had been created that gave me clues to my past that could help me for my future.

This simple exercise allowed me to see my life in a way that helped me understand my career and the decisions that I had made. A theme developed: running away. More than running away, I seemed to run away and end up with the same result: unhappiness.

Ran away after college. I wanted to get the heck away from the Midwest to begin my life in a place where I could come out of the closet and finally be me.

	WHAT DID I ENJOY ABOUT THE POSITION	WHAT WAS MY FAVORITE MEMORY	WHAT DID I NOT ENJOY	WHAT... HAPPENING IN MY PERSONAL LIFE	GRADE
nue for Gatorade, Sales Strategy to Created post-event cross-functional ge by 76% (from o Analysts.	• CLOSER TO FAMILY • DIVESE COMPANY	• WORKING FOR DIVERSE COMPANY • JOINING EMPLOYEE RESOURCE GROUP • WORKED WITH GATORADE	• BOSS WAS MICRO-MANAGER • PRESSURE • DIDN'T KNOW FUNCTION VERY WELL	• CAME OUT AT WORK • BEGAN DATING • STRUGGLING WITH COLD WEATHER • SAW FAMILY MORE OFTEN	D+
2006~2011 ith consumers tegies to senior is for growth and cial solutions to solving complex ulting team.	• BECAME YOUNGEST DIRECTOR • NO FLORIDA INCOME TAX • BUILDING STRATEGY FOR COMPANY • IN SENIOR LEADERSHIP MEETINGS	• TRAVEL ACROSS COUNTRY	• TERMINATING FRANCHISE OWNERS • BEING IN THE CLOSET	• NO ONE TO DATE • GOT MY MBA • MOM DIVORCED MY DAD • DAD THINKS DEVIL LIVES INSIDE OF ME • SISTER DIVORCED HER HUSBAND	C+
d with franchise profitability.	• ENJOYED HELPING BUSINESS OWNERS • SOLVED PROBLEMS	• BUILDING RELATIONSHIPS WITH CUSTOMERS • TURNED AROUND BUSINESS	• WORKING FOR SMALL, PRIVATE COMPANY • NO DIVERSITY	• LIVING IN FLORIDA • IN CLOSET AT WORK	C+
2004~2006 demographics employees.	• I WAS IN-CHARGE • LEARNING OTHER SKILLS BESIDES FINANCE • WORK/LIFE FLEXIBILITY	• GOING INTO WORK WHENEVER I WANTED	• NOT GETTING PAID • THE OWNER HAD A LAWSUIT	• STRUGGLING WITH COMING OUT TO EVERYONE • BURNT OUT OF NYC	C-
2001~2004 00 employees financial models.	• MONEY • BUILDING FINANCIAL MODELS	• CLOSING/PRICING MULTI-MILLION DOLLAR DEALS • FUN DINNERS WITH TEAM	• 90+ HOURS/WEEK	• STRUGGLING WITH DATING • PARTYING IN NYC	C
t rate swaps and ivatives team.	• MONEY • PRESTIGE	• BEING SELECTED AS TOP ANALYST	• HAD NO IDEA WHAT I WAS DOING • TEAM OF A-HOLES	• 9/11 • COMING OUT TO MYSELF/FAMILY	D-

'My 2-column resume'

Ran away after investment banking. I wanted to get the heck away from 90- to 100-hour work weeks. But I had no idea what I wanted to do, so I took a month-long trip round the world. When I returned, I would take on various things like work for a presidential campaign, work for a dot.com pet project for the first openly gay person on the New York Stock Exchange, and eventually obtain my real estate license.

Ran away after New York City. I wanted to get the heck away from the Big Apple since I was floating and not generating any income.

Ran away after Florida. I wanted to get the heck out of a slowly dying industry and out of a place where my dating life was non-existent.

Ran away after New York City part 2. I wanted to run away for good. Away from my career. Away from my ex-boyfriend. Away from the city that was good for me in my 20s but exhausting for me in my 30s.

I still had no idea what I wanted to do with my life, and even after all this running, changing jobs, and tweaking resumes, I still wasn't happy.

I was always running to get away from something I didn't love. When things became too hard to manage, I ran away instead of really digging deep to understand the root of the issue.

My gut was screaming so loudly to find a new path, but because I didn't know how, I would just run. Unbeknownst to me, I was just running farther down the same path. I wasn't jumping to a new one. I couldn't see that the corporate world was the common denominator.

I fell into the trap over and over. There were times in my career I felt like I finally landed a job that would prevent me from running away. Working for Gatorade, a company owned by PepsiCo, was my dream come true. Working for an iconic brand in an international capacity in the strategy function would make me happy—or so I thought.

However, there were many days when I loved going into the office building knowing I worked for Gatorade, but when I got to my desk, I didn't really want to be doing what I was supposed to be doing, which was paying advertising bills and managing the budget for our team. I was really good at doing this, but it wasn't something I loved to do.

I was now in what I considered to be my dream job, so my unhappiness was baffling. This is where the right side of my resume would have been so important. While the left side of my resume looked impressive and successful, I didn't feel happy.

I figured I was the problem, not the job—after all, I seemed like I had it made. The job paid well. I had great benefits. The office was only a mile from the condo I had purchased, so I walked to work when the weather was nice. On days it wasn't nice, I hopped on a convenient bus route that picked me up a block away from my condo and dropped me off a block from work. The office had a gym on the top floor with a greatly reduced price where I could exercise during work hours if I didn't have anything going on. It was what other people dreamed of having.

Others saw me as successful. I had everything I needed, but something continued to tell me that there is more to life than this. I felt locked in. I couldn't help but think that the career path I was on would never provide internal happiness, peace, or fulfillment.

I felt trapped that I had to go to the same office every day. I would arrive at work and look out at the window wishing I were outside doing something else. I was good at finance, but I got bored with finance. I felt my personality had adjusted to not wanting to be behind the scenes, but more on the front lines. In front of the customer, or finding ways to attract new customers. That was all well and good, but despite it all, I wanted something else. My mind would spin trying really hard to figure out what that "something else" I wanted so badly was, but I couldn't come up with anything.

THE HIDDEN COLUMN

As the years went on, I wanted to use my creative mind more and more. I needed a challenge, so I used my international finance and strategy role to land a corporate strategy job at PepsiCo's World Headquarters.

Again, my ego was so proud. I was "big time." Now living in New York City again, Director of Global Strategy for all beverages worldwide. I had climbed the corporate ladder and was creating presentations for the CEO of PepsiCo. Maybe this was my dream job? It certainly would be considered a dream job to my peers.

But if I were to fill out the right side of my resume with my emotions and feelings, it would look like this:

- I am unhappy in my current relationship. Even though my boyfriend lives in New York and now I just moved to New York, I don't want to live with him because I am concerned he is not the one.
- Even though I can work out of the more convenient Soho location on Fridays (instead of driving an hour up to the World Headquarters north of Manhattan), I don't want to travel to an office to work each day, no matter where it is.
- I often feel confused and dumb working with such brilliant people. Yes, I surrounded myself with people smarter than me, but I often feel like a fish out of water since my colleagues spent their careers in strategy roles, whereas I came from more of an operational background.
- I often—sometimes more than once a day— dream about going out to see the world. Three weeks of vacation is not enough for me.
- The work I do seems important, but doesn't feel important to me.
- I want to work for myself. I don't like working for someone else's agenda.

- I have a passion to help others. While I am fulfilled with my work leading the Global LGBT group, my gay job, I don't feel fulfilled in my day job.
- I want to have flexibility to live where I want to live.

The right side of my resume began filling up quickly with many emotions that aren't seen or felt while reading the left side. It opened my eyes to see just *how* awful I was feeling every day.

Writing the right side of my resume is something I had never done, or even thought to do. This was an exercise that I only did after years and years of unhappiness that finally led to leaving my corporate career. I can only imagine what I would have done if I had really listened to my emotions earlier in my career.

Sitting by the pool far away from home finally taking a deeper look into my career on a more holistic level, I graded my current job. And after taking this hidden column of my resume into account, I got a D+. Not a failure, but definitely nothing to write home about. I was passing, but barely scraping by.

Did I really want to live a "D+" life?

CAREER DNA

The right side of my resume held so many facts and emotions I had previously thrown under a rug, thinking "I'll deal with that some other time." I did notice those thoughts and emotions, and while at times I changed jobs or moved to a new city as a result, I did not take the time to fully understand these thoughts and emotions. It was almost like the emotions were so powerful that I could only react to them quickly, instead of sitting down to build a way out.

Reacting like this to big thoughts and emotions is common. We see something and it is easier to rely on our knee-jerk reaction instead of taking the time to assess what's happening. If I would have performed this right-side resume exercise ten years ago, I would have pulled out the following:

- I love helping other people become the best version of themselves
- I want to create a product I own and provides true value for others
- I want to have a lifestyle where I can be anywhere in the world at any time
- I am successful, and I will be successful no matter what I do when I truly believe in something

- I don't want to work for someone else, especially someone who is not inspiring to me on a daily basis

This career roadmap not only helped me see where I was most unhappy throughout my career, but it also quickly showed me where I was the happiest in my life. It wasn't the corporate work that I was performing each day to help the company sell more cans of soda or more bottles of water. I loved my gay job more than my day job when I led the global LGBT resource group at PepsiCo. My happiest moments were helping others become their authentic selves in and out of the workplace.

HOW WOULD I MAKE MONEY DOING SOMETHING I LOVE?

At the moment when I realized how much I loved my gay job, I thought (briefly), how can I make money doing what I love to do? I researched diversity consulting firms and inquired how I could become a part of one...or create my own business.

The idea to create my own consulting firm seemed so daunting. I saw many others in this space helping companies to create a more inclusive and diverse work environment. And it scared me to see how many people were doing this because it would be too difficult to stand out in a crowded space. In fact, it quickly squashed these hopes and I threw that dream out the window.

How often do we do this to ourselves? How often do you have a dream "I would love to do that someday" only to have unanswerable questions pop up and eventually squash your dream? Questions and thoughts like:

1. How would I make money doing this?
2. How would I support my family?
3. There are many competitors, how would I be able to stand out?
4. I've never started anything before, I don't know where to begin.
5. The idea sounds great, but the steps seem too difficult to create something like this.
6. My education is in this specific field; if I change, then it feels like I am starting over at my age and that is scary.
7. This career is more than a career, it's a huge part of my identity. People count on me. Would I be letting them down?
8. I helped build this program/business/culture, how can I just walk away?

When I left my corporate job, I had no idea what I wanted to do. After spending time away and letting my mind heal, everything began to appear clearly. My higher purpose. My mission. What I want to do with my life. How I will make money. You can do this, too. Going after your dream will produce a happier and wealthier life than remaining on the traditional path, a chosen path of not taking any risks based on the fear of failure.

Your past jobs and experiences are like your career DNA. It will give you clues to help you not only figure out what you have enjoyed in the past, but also what you have not enjoyed throughout your career. And it will help you uncover how your personal life may have impacted your career in different ways. Use this knowledge as a starting point to your future roadmap and your ultimate life success.

Now it's your turn:
- ❑ Pull out your resume and ask yourself:
    - ❑ What did I enjoy (not enjoy) about each position?
    - ❑ What was occurring in my life at that time?
    - ❑ What were my fears, my struggles, my happiness level?
- ❑ Does a pattern appear?
- ❑ Did your personal life impact your professional life (or vice versa)?

ONLINE EXERCISE

Go to "Chapter 5 - Lesson 2: Write Your 2-Column Resume" of the *Jump Without A Parachute Companion Course* at **JUMPWITHOUTAPARACHUTE.COM/ COURSE** and download a free template that you can print out to complete your personal 2-column resume.

LESSON 3:
JUMP WITHOUT
A PARACHUTE

ALL THE ANSWERS

While still unhappily employed, once the "What do I want to do with the rest of my life?" question overtook my mind, I couldn't be content until I could figure out the answer.

I had many interests, but the concept of working for someone else on someone else's time was no longer an option. So, what was it I really wanted?

- To work from anywhere in the world at any time. I didn't want to have to be tied to one location.
- To see the world—as much as I could, when I wanted to, without permission from someone else.
- To build something of my own. To know that I was responsible for the success or failure of *my* company.
- To have an income trajectory UPSIDE greater than I would have following the corporate path, which is mostly capped (within a certain range).

But the most important thing I needed was to be fulfilled each day of my life. I needed work to no longer be something I had to do, but something I wanted to do.

After breaking up with my ex-boyfriend, I turned the vacation we had planned into a two-week solo trip to Bali. My body drenched in sweat after a detoxifying vinyasa class at the world-famous Yoga Barn in Ubud, I sat down at a picnic table to refuel. On the other side of the table was a French woman, Camille, from Paris who looked to be about the same age as me. She was writing in her journal.

After writing a long stream of consciousness, she quietly looked up and our eyes met. Her face softened as she said hello and we began chatting about where we were from.

I don't believe in accidents in life. I believe that everything is given to us at the perfect moment, even when sometimes it doesn't feel that way. Camille told me how she left her 16-year corporate marketing career six months prior, packed all of her belongings in a storage unit, and flew to Bali to begin pursuing her passion to become a yoga instructor.

After explaining my story to her and explaining how "stuck" I felt, she smiled at me and said "just jump."

That was the thing: I was ready to jump, but I wanted to make sure I knew all of the answers to all of my questions. These would be the answers I needed to land softly after jumping. I certainly did not want to crash land.

I wanted to know exactly what I would be doing to make money, receive health benefits, and save for retirement. I didn't want to give up my incredible salary or years of my hard work building my impressive resume and climbing the corporate ladder to become a Director of a Fortune 50 company. I also didn't want to give up all of the almost guaranteed financial comfort of climbing higher on the ladder. The prestige. The lifestyle. The corporate treasure hunt!

I wanted to know I would be okay. If we all knew with 100% certainty that we would be 100% happy and have all of the resources to live our desired lifestyle through our death date, we all would choose that path! None of us would choose 50% happiness for the rest of our lives. If you would, then why have you read this far?

Just Jump. How freeing does that sound? I looked at Camille with curiosity as my small grin shifted into a wider smile. The hundreds of thousands of nerves lining my stomach were cheering. They finally heard what they had been trying to tell me all along.

Someone had essentially given me permission to do what I wanted. It was validation to move forward without knowing all the answers. Other people have gone before me and they are okay. It wasn't reckless. It was calculated. It was intelligent. But most of all, it was freeing.

After a brief pause, with energy flowing through my body, I said to Camille, "I'm scared, but I know that's what I need to do. I know that I would regret it the rest of my life if I never tried. I would always wonder 'what if,' and that would kill me. I am a smart guy. I know I will figure it out."

JUMP WITHOUT THE ANSWERS

Monday morning at 3am, the day I returned from my two-week trip to Bali, my eyes flipped open and I swiftly sat up in bed. Camille's words had been echoing in my head ever since she said them.

"Just jump. Jump without a parachute," I told myself out loud as the light from the city below dimly lit my room. "You will figure out how to land. Just like you always have. You landed a job on Wall Street from Ball State. You landed a successful consulting gig after moving to Florida with no job. You have found success in your life before. And you will find success again. You will find a way to land safely."

I finally understood I couldn't have one foot in the door and one foot out of the door to figure out what I wanted to do with the rest of my life. I had to exit the room completely. And I had to close that door and proceed down the pitch-black hallway before I could even locate the next room to enter.

This is the only way to figure it out. I needed to be all in!

Go back to a time in your life where you didn't know what to expect, yet you found your way out. You have already proven you can succeed when you aren't quite sure of the exact answer. While it may not have worked out according to the plan you had in mind, you found another way to make that okay.

Jumping without a parachute is the same thing. It requires you to venture into the unknown. Into a place where the answers aren't immediately clear. You may not know where your next paycheck will come from, or exactly what you will be doing.

When you jump without the answers, you are forced to figure them all out as you go. And this is where the magic happens. This journey will have more of an impact on your life than staying in an unhappy situation. I have learned through my experience that even if you come up against tough roadblocks on your journey, you will find a way to overcome them, because you have to.

When people say "But I don't know what I want to do," it typically means that they aren't willing to go try something new. When you say, "I don't know what I want to do," you aren't moving. You're standing still.

Once you start moving, the possibilities are endless. You may not always know where you're headed; however, any movement is *learning*. This learning is finding your way toward what you want to do. You must take the first step before you can take your second and third and eventually move down a new path.

The beauty of jumping into the unknown is that you must keep an open mind to what happens. Along this journey, things will happen to you that you could have never expected. And that is what makes your life rich.

MONEY IS NOT THE ANSWER

To jump without a parachute, you must first realize money is not the answer. For years, money was the thing that held me back. The necessity of money comes in different forms. Housing payments. Lifestyle habits, like clothing and lattes and nightclubs and eating out. Children (no, I'm not saying children are a problem. Using children as an excuse to not follow your passion is the issue. "I have a family to support.").

Each person comes from a different family structure, but money plays some sort of role in every family's lifestyle. Some families came from abundance, some came from a life not attached to money, and some families live with a scarcity mentality.

If you came from an upbringing where money equaled status and you felt you must maintain a certain status with your social circle, then money will play a much more dominant role in your life. It will influence your decisions about your lifestyle and career. And if you grew up in a family where money was scarce, your decisions about money and saving could impact your risk tolerance in all areas of your life, including your career.

However, to ultimately become happy, one must let go of feelings about money. This doesn't mean that money is not important or is not needed to sustain a certain lifestyle. Money too often has influence over our career decisions and leads us to unhappiness. Only when we let go of money as an influence in our life can we truly be free to not worry about how we will make money, how we will receive health benefits, and how we will save for retirement.

The answers to all of those questions are the parachute that allows your mind to be comforted before and after you jump. Those "known answers" are the parachute strings for an easy descent and soft landing. Our mind seems to require those answers before jumping, which is why most people will never jump. Most people want the answer before making the leap. But the answer lives in the freefall. The moment we take action is the moment we begin to find our way.

For many, making the leap without the answers is something they would never do. However, think about the flip side: What does your life look like if you never jump because you don't have the answers? What does your happiness look like and for how long will that level of happiness last? Is that period of your life, that percentage of your life, worth it to stay in comfort or even to be controlled by an unhappy job?

This is not an easy step, but I wrote this book to help you save time. It took me ten years to finally realize what was holding me back. It was money all along. I would convince myself I loved my job because of the money, benefits, and perks (which, I later realized, were all basically just money).

I had reverse-engineered my thinking to adapt happiness to money. I trained myself to do this over years and years of thinking this way until it became "natural." We all do this to a certain degree.

We all know in our guts what the answer is, but we aren't trained to jump. It goes against everything we have been taught. Graduate, get a job, work that job, get a better job, retire. No space for jumping in that formula!

However, after years and years of going around in unhappy circles of meaningless change, money, comfort, unhappiness, etc., I became smart enough to realize that this cycle is not what I want. I had to stop equating money to happiness.

I realize that some of you may be saying, "But Cory, I need money to literally survive. I require insurance to pay for medications and healthcare for a specific medical condition." I'm not asking you to be reckless and quit your job without sensible consideration of next steps. I'm asking you to consider making an adjustment to your unhappy career situation, which could mean shifting positions within your company. Get creative and use the lessons in this book to adapt to your situation without putting your own life at risk.

(We will cover all kinds of excuses and statements we often use to prevent ourselves from jumping in Chapters 9-11: Get Out of Your Own Way.)

As much as I was waiting for all the answers to appear, I had to jump without parachute strings supporting me on the way down. I had to go out and find the answers during the journey. I never would have found them while still following my corporate path because I never had the time or mental bandwidth to figure it out. You must step out of your comfort zone to find the answer. And the only way to do that is to jump without knowing all of the answers and trust you will land. Because you will, just like you always have before.

Now it's your turn:
- ❑ What are your parachute strings?
- ❑ What would you have to believe to cut the strings?
- ❑ What would happen if you never jumped?

ONLINE EXERCISE

Go to "Chapter 6 - Lesson 3: Jump Without A Parachute" of the *Jump Without A Parachute Companion Course* at **JUMPWITHOUTAPARACHUTE. COM/COURSE** and complete the exercise to help you understand your "jumping" scenarios.

LESSON 4:
TAKE TIME TO THINK

After assessing my two-column resume, it didn't take long to see how unhappy I was.

Why was I doing all of this if I was not happy?

I could continue to say to myself, "I don't know what I want to do with the rest of my life" while following my learned path, or I could finally take the time to figure it out. But when? And how?

I could take a one- to two-week vacation to focus on planning the rest of my life. But I knew how difficult it is to try to use time away for brain power when my mind needed a rest. It was so hard to just stop and think about all of this. No wonder most people simply don't.

My gut was telling me something different all along. My gut was telling me that the corporate world was not for me.

A week or two away wasn't going to be enough. That became clear as my time in Bali came to an end. So I decided not only to leave my job but also to leave my corporate career path altogether.

The day I returned to work after my two-week vacation, I had no doubts anymore. I describe this story in detail in my memoir, *I Almost Became Me,* but in the early hours before returning to work, I dug into the bowels of my company's corporate policies and learned of an obscure benefit that very few ever take advantage of: "Leave of Absence."

I learned my company allowed me to take up to six months of unpaid time away from my job (there were specific requirements, like having been with the company for more than a year and also having my manager approve it). However, I was able to retain my corporate health benefits at the same cost I was paying. And I had the option to return to my existing job.

My manager and human resources contact approved my leave and three weeks later, I completed my last day of my corporate job for a while—I originally thought. I broke my two-year lease, packed all my belongings into a storage unit, and set out on an adventure that would change my life forever.

My plan was to travel the world, first visiting Antarctica, then hopping over to New Zealand and Australia before making my way through Southeast Asia.

It wasn't until I left that I realized how important time away truly is—and I mean *unlimited* time away. I finally had time to think. Time to breathe. Time to focus on myself without feeling like there was something else I was supposed to be doing.

It was two to three months into my time away from the corporate environment before I could finally begin to relax. This didn't mean my mind was ready to think, just that my mind was ready to relax. That is how long it takes to be at the starting point of your journey. Your mind needs time to unwind and begin living. I don't think I was truly living before that all happened. I was existing on the path I was taught to follow.

While I had known for a while I wasn't fulfilled in the corporate world, the moment my mind fully relaxed was the moment I realized I could no longer go back. It felt like I finally had the correct prescription for my eyeglasses. Before, I was straining to figure out my life and I was so confused why it wasn't easier. Everything in my life was blurry. But once my mind calmed down enough to focus, I could see perfectly and all of the colors shined through brilliantly. I was finally seeing life at 20/20.

I continued traveling the world. I never went back to my job or my career again.

It wasn't until a full year after I left the corporate world when my mind had enough time to eventually figure out what I wanted to do.

Now you may be sitting there thinking: one year? I can't take a full year off... How will I make money?

Ah, yes, the mental chatter pops back again. The mental chatter we are so good at. The mental chatter that continues to hold us back and keeps us in an unhappy state. There is a reason very few people ever make this leap.

Our minds do not like this level of discomfort. These thoughts of "how" and "I can't" quickly take us back to our autopilot. Our place of comfort. Our path to our lame retirement party after 35 years in the same cubicle.

Your mind requires time away to unwind, because our minds hold space for the responsibilities we have created for ourselves. Remember, the only thing we really have in life is time. Take away all of our possessions, our career, other people, and what do we have left? Time. A finite amount of time. We each have 24 hours in a day, 7 days in a week, 52 weeks in a year, and hopefully a good 80 to 90 years (or more) of life.

It comes down to how you fill up that time. If your job prevents you from spending time doing something you love, then maybe it is time to recalibrate the amount of time you spend doing what you don't love to do.

Find time to focus on the rest of your life. Here are some things to consider:

1. If you can afford to do it, leave your current situation altogether. This is the best option that allows the most freedom for your mind to think clearly. You will be able to unwind the tethers that have held you back.

2. If you aren't ready to leave your job but you can afford to do it, ask your employer to take a sabbatical.

3. If a sabbatical or "Leave of Absence" does not exist at your company, create one. Many resources exist online outlining how to ask your employer to take an extended amount of time away from your job.

4. If you cannot afford to leave your job or take an unpaid leave of absence, the following are options for you. These options are not conducive to providing an adequate amount of mental space needed to discover your new path, but at the very least, if these are your only options, you will be able to begin the journey of figuring it out— which is better than not figuring it out.

   a) Stay in your current job but carve out mental space and time to focus on your future.

This sounds easy, but is very difficult to do. Remember, I tried to do this for years, but my job took up a large amount of my mental capacity that left me too exhausted to figure out my life.

b) Leave your current job that is making you unhappy and find a temporary job that pays your bills and benefits but allows you time to think clearer without much distraction. Use this only if your current job doesn't allow you time to think clearly or monopolizes your mental capacity. As I have explained in the previous chapters, most corporate jobs don't allow you the mind space to think about many other things. Be very careful with this option

5. If you have an idea of a career you want to pursue, consider enrolling into a full-time or part-time higher education program (either in person or online). Some companies offer tuition reimbursement, which you may be able to take advantage of.

6. Pursue a passion or hobby to learn something new that would create potential for growth. This could open up possibilities within or outside of your current career.

The goal with these options is to allow yourself as much time as possible, so you are able to really step back and think more holistically about your life and career. Giving yourself and your mind time to think will set you up for future success. Think of it as the foundation to your life. You must pour the foundation before you can build on top of it.

It is important to rest your mind. You most likely will need more than a week or two of vacation to go figure it all out. In the online *Companion Course,* I've created an exercise and template for you to download for this chapter that will help you build your own personal road-map to take the time you need for your mind to relax long enough for you to focus your brain power on what you want to do. This exercise will help you organize your thoughts and help create a plan so it isn't overwhelming.

Take the time you need to think. Don't try to shortcut this. Take as long as you can. While you may not know how much you will need, take at least three months to start.

If you want something badly enough, you will do it.

Now it's your turn:
- ❑ How will you find time to relax and calm your mind?
- ❑ Can you take extended leave from your current position?

❑ Does your company offer you a Leave of Absence or sabbatical? If not, could you create one?

ONLINE EXERCISE

Go to "Chapter 7 - Lesson 4: Take Time To Think" of the *Jump Without A Parachute Companion Course* at **JUMPWITHOUTAPARACHUTE.COM/COURSE** and get ready to create your roadmap toward quieting your mind.

LESSON 5:
LEARN HOW TO FAIL

UNLEARN WHAT YOU'VE LEARNED

Almost one year to the day after that first Monday morning back to work after returning from my Bali vacation when I realized I needed to leave the corporate world for good, it hit me while I was flying at 30,000 feet between Iceland and England. I was staring out of the window and my idea just snapped into my mind: combine the things you love in your life—travel and helping other people—and create a business opportunity around this idea.

It seems I could have easily come up with the idea years ago. But I had to go through the journey to allow my mind the time to reset, to have the space available to think clearly, and to build confidence that I can actually go out on my own and create something.

I set out to create Pivot Trip, a company that leads holistic and immersive global experiences in exotic parts of the world designed to empower participants toward extraordinary life success and ultimate inner happiness.

Not only was my dream coming true, but I also felt empowered. I was creating my own company and the concept was crystal clear in my mind after taking the time to think during the previous year. It made me happy to have the opportunity to facilitate positive change in people's lives. My gut agreed. There was no doubt that this was my path. It was my opportunity to blaze my own trail to personal happiness and fulfillment.

But now that I had created my concept, I needed to prove it was viable. So I began building my first retreat from scratch.

It quickly became apparent that I had to unlearn what I had learned in the corporate world. And by unlearning, I don't mean forgetting. However, small, startup businesses operate in a much different way than a large corporation.

"Well, duh!" you may be saying right now. It seems obvious. It seemed obvious to me at the time, too, but I immediately hit roadblocks. I was used to planning the best strategy, then relying on the operations, sales, and marketing teams to execute the plan. I was now the strategist, planner, operations person, salesperson, and marketing person. If I had a question along the way, there was no specialized team around me. I had to go figure it out on my own.

Within a corporation, I spent time maneuvering through a specific set of rules and guidelines. Policies, procedures, protocols, and hierarchies added layers to my work. This allowed for lower levels of productivity as a percentage of output because everyone became accustomed to projects and processes taking a long time. I only had to worry about playing my part within my function in the overall process. I learned to let the process control me.

Throw all of this out the window as an entrepreneur. I could no longer think the same way I did when I had the security of others operating close to me. Now it was just me. As an entrepreneur, you wear all of the hats. You must find a way to succeed on your own. If you don't do something, the process does not move. And guess what: when you have to find a way to do everything on your own, you are bound to fail.

Which is another thing you must unlearn: That failure is bad.

I heard countless times within the walls of the corporations I worked for that it's ok to fail, as long as you don't fail on the same thing twice. While employees hear that failure is okay, they also hear they can't fail often. If they do fail often, those employees are slowly "transitioned out of the company." Companies incentivize fast learners, for sure.

One of the most important lessons I have learned as an entrepreneur is that failure while trying something new is the second-most-important part of success. The first is learning from that failure, and making your product/service/business even better. You can't have learning without failing. They go hand in hand.

Unfortunately, at a corporation or larger organization, learning to fail is limited because of its structure and hierarchy. In fact, failure is frowned upon. Multiple layers have been created to ultimately monitor and improve productivity. Each employee ID number has a specific task to perform to ensure the corporate machine operates at the optimal level. When the optimal level has not been achieved, this failure can be a sign of an employee not doing their job well.

However, when you fail, you learn. And when you learn, you find new (often better) ways to succeed. This is one of the true paths to accomplishing a goal.

Let's dive deeper into failure. First, we must understand the difference between losing and failure, because we often associate the two words with each other. However, the words have very different meanings and extremely different impacts on the choices we make in life.

Remember the entire concept about learning the path we are currently on from our influencers?

When we are younger, we experience many losses. We lost sporting events or we lost at the board game we were playing (except for Monopoly), or we didn't get the part in the school play, or we didn't get our own way within a group. At the time, these losses were devastating. It temporarily seemed that our world would end. But minutes, hours, or days later, we seemed to forget about the loss.

We moved on, and our influencers (hopefully) encouraged us to keep trying. To keep doing better. They told us it was okay to lose. They understood there was learning in losing. Losses occur, but they seem temporary.

Failure carries more weight than loss. Failure feels more permanent. It seems to carry more shame and even makes us feel unworthy to ourselves and to others.

These so-called failures can take the form of big events like not getting into the school of your choice, not passing a huge test that allows you into a special program, not getting the job that you think you are qualified for, or not being where you hoped you would be at a specific point in your life.

These deeper forms of loss impact us in a much bigger way—a way that we remember longer, and sometimes never are able to forget. When we were younger, our influencers were there to show empathy and help us learn that losing was okay. But when these failures occur later in life, who is there to help us through?

When we are younger, it is easier for us to bounce back from a loss. As we age, however, it seems we are not as flexible to adjust.

For some reason we think failure is something we cannot face. It is something that needs to be avoided at all costs. But why?

Because it is what we have been trained to do. We have been trained to try to win. Many of us have trained ourselves to only make decisions that will have positive outcomes. Said another way, we only make decisions to avoid a negative outcome.

Our brains have been trained to seek comfort, and winning feels comfortable. The potential of failure, even if it may bring with it new solutions, is not comfortable. We don't want to have to deal with struggle or pain or hurt. We don't want the loss. If we invest the time and energy to try something new, we don't want the risk of failure.

That's why so few of us jump without a parachute.

WORST-CASE SCENARIO

What are your initial feelings when reading these questions?

1. If I quit my job today, what would I do to make money?
2. If I quit my job today, how would I pay my bills and live a comfortable life in retirement?

Now read these statements, and note your initial feelings.

1. When I quit my job today, I will find a way to make money.
2. When I quit my job today, I will be able to pay my bills and live comfortably in retirement.

Did you experience a different feeling after reading these two groups of statements and questions?

In the first group, the questions elicit the unknown. The answers may be hard to think about (and seem downright scary). However, the second group of statements provides comfort, knowing everything will be all right.

When we don't know the answers or are presented with an overwhelming decision, our minds do a great job of filling in everything bad that can happen. Our minds, always seeking comfort, have been trained to think of the worst-case scenario to prevent ourselves from taking the risks associated with the situation. Which means, once we come up with the worst case, we begin telling ourselves that risking it is not a good option. The idea of failure creeps in and we talk ourselves out of trying.

However, when we acknowledge we don't know the answers but believe we will find an answer that will work for us, we feel much better about it. The idea of failing doesn't creep into our minds. We know it may not be easy, but we are more inclined to try.

WHAT IS THE WORST THING THAT WILL HAPPEN?

When we are confronted with a complex situation, it can be difficult for us to see a clear path through it.

When I first began daydreaming about leaving my career and traveling the world, the euphoric feelings of being free overwhelmed me. I envisioned myself on a remote beach in Thailand, free of worries from my job and career, but still living in pure comfort.

I began thinking through everything I would need to do to make that daydream a reality. I first would need to leave my job. That was the easy part. Then I'd begin planning a trip. That was the fun part. I envisioned myself finally arriving and just soaking it all in for two to three weeks. Ah, pure bliss.

And then, guess what happened? Guess where my mind very quickly shifted to?

How would you afford to continue traveling? What would you do to make money? How would you save for retirement? And on and on and on until my mind began thinking how I would lose all of my money, not be able to afford healthcare, and how I would be forced to live back home with my family in rural Ohio as a single gay man at 50 years old.

My mind froze, overwhelmed. I was terrified of becoming such a monumental failure, but I only became so terrified because I was trying to solve very big questions in a daydream. This is a recipe for the daydream to instantly shut off. My eyes went back to the snow falling outside of the office window at 3pm on a Tuesday afternoon.

My mind went to a bleak space. The daydream quashed. The worst-case scenario seemed inevitable: if I take that risk, I will lose gigantically. However, in retrospect, it was a giant overreaction. Basically homeless and forced to live with family members at 50 years old. Really?

See, that is the thing with our minds. There will always be a worst-case scenario. We allow our minds to let the small chance of that worst case happening control our actions.

But what about the best-case scenario? I allowed myself the time to think and daydream without limits… I was creating an incredible company, turning my passion into a viable business opportunity that helped other people. I was no longer waking up to an alarm, but beginning to earn more than enough to support a comfortable lifestyle for my family. I was free to be wherever I wanted to be in the world, and I was preparing for a comfortable life when I plan to slow down. Turns out, this was the path my life ended up taking, but my daydream didn't even consider the better case as a possibility.

Let's walk through the worst-case scenario to provide an example of what would actually happen: I begin traveling the world on my savings. I have some incredible experiences that will last a lifetime and I realize I need to figure out how to offset my travel expenses. I realize that I have numerous business and personal skills that I have learned throughout my life that I can use to earn some income. I seek out ways that I can use my skills while still traveling and enjoying my life. While I won't make the same salary that I was making when I left, I will begin earning enough to offset my costs.

Over time, because I am an intelligent human being, I figure out how to earn income without compromising my happiness. Then the possibilities become endless. Maybe

I will meet someone and that takes priority. Maybe I start up a business that I become passionate about and dive in. Maybe I am content earning enough to cover my living expenses and saving up for other things I want in the future.

The worst-case scenario is just another thing our brains use as an excuse to keep us in comfort and stop us from taking a risk. The worst-case scenario most likely will never happen. In fact, what will actually happen will likely be very far from the worst possible thing.

Here is the most important part: by taking this risk, you will learn more about yourself than you would have by not taking the risk. Which means your life will be better off as a result of taking the risk.

The upside is even greater by following your passion. You could end up in a situation you never knew was possible, a situation you never knew existed. There is no limit to the upside of following your passion.

But on the flip side, when you don't follow your passion, your upside is capped because you are still doing the same things that don't make you happy. Your situation will always stay mostly the same. You may have a little upside, but that upside is limited.

Our minds are trained to overvalue the worst case on the scale of "what ifs." We think, "I don't have this talent, therefore I can't." If our gut is telling us something, why don't we trust ourselves to find a way to obtain what we don't have?

What if you tried to pursue something and ended up with your worst-case scenario? Were you pursuing a true passion, or were you chasing a superficial outcome like fame, followers, or money? When you pursue something to satisfy a deep, inner desire, you will find a way to your destination, and the worst-case scenario most likely will be avoided as a result.

It reminds me of the childhood song *The Hokey Pokey*. "You put your whole self in." If you don't put your whole self in, then you are setting yourself up to achieve lackluster results.

Remember to use these moments of failure as an opportunity. Ask yourself:

- What specifically did not work out?
- What skills did I obtain from this experience?
- How can I apply these learnings and skills to pursue a passion?
- How can I share these learnings with others?

We become what we believe in our minds. If our minds convince us we are limited in our potential, then our life outcome will be limited. When we believe we will fail, we will fail. When we believe we will succeed, we will succeed.

While it may appear that some people are luckier than others, I believe they prepared themselves to be in the right place at the right time. You may have heard the quote attributed to Roman philosopher Seneca, "Luck is what happens when preparation meets opportunity." You must buy a lottery ticket in order to win. You need to place yourself in a position of success in order to succeed.

I also understand many people are born into a family or situation that creates more (or less) opportunity than many others. However, the same principle applies to all scenarios. Others may have specific advantages (or disadvantages), but our thoughts will be the ultimate determinant to success. Some may have to work harder than others to achieve success, but the rewards will be sweeter.

You can begin to train your mind to believe these statements by unlearning what you have learned. We must unlearn our thought patterns that led us to dwelling on the worst-case scenario. We must unlearn that failure is a bad thing. We must unlearn that money is the definition of success.

Now it's your turn:
- ❑ What do you need to unlearn for you to find a new, happy path?
- ❑ Identify a moment in your life when something did not turn out the way that you hoped it would (i.e. job

you did not get, business you did not obtain, etc.). Think of the positive outcomes that resulted. In what ways did you grow mentally and emotionally from this experience?

❏ What situation have you been procrastinating on or holding back from?

    ❏ What is the worst-case outcome if you did what you haven't done yet?

    ❏ What is the best-case outcome?

    ❏ What is the likely outcome?

ONLINE EXERCISE

Go to "Chapter 8 - Lesson 5: Learn How To Fail" of the *Jump Without A Parachute Companion Course* at **JUMPWITHOUTAPARACHUTE.COM/COURSE** and get ready to take some risks!

PART 3: JUMP

GET OUT OF
YOUR OWN WAY:
MONEY WORRIES

When faced with a complex task, have you ever unequivocally known what you need to do and maybe you even knew how to do what you needed to do, but you just didn't do it? And we aren't talking about how you know you need to do the laundry today but you just don't do it. We are talking about a life goal, like pursuing a fulfilling career.

You know you need to listen to your gut. You know you need to jump without a parachute. You just haven't done it yet.

Remember how our brains don't want to be disrupted? In situations like these, your brain is saying "Nope, I am doing just fine as I am now."

We don't want to have to go through the mental acrobatics trying to figure out how to successfully complete the task, nor face any potential negative consequences that will come along with completing the task. When something seems too complex or we can't visualize a clear path to the final result, guess what happens?

We procrastinate!

However, you most likely already have everything you need to transform your life. What I have found through coaching others is usually there is only one thing in your way: YOU!

I can hear you now: "Sure! All of this makes complete sense. It is the perfect world where you can just quit your job and take the time you need to build a roadmap to live your passions and dreams every day."

And then, that three-letter word comes up so quickly: But....

We have trained our brains to use this three-letter word as a defense mechanism, shielding the voice of our gut. That "but" is then followed by a phrase that your brain insists is logical, when you know it's actually based in fear.

There are certainly real-life consequences to jumping without a parachute. However, I will dive into these situations to show that it isn't as bad as you think. I want to show how you can rewire your brain to think about the positive consequences and focus on "what's possible?" instead of shutting down the thought the moment it seems difficult.

There are many ways to transform your life and career, like shifting into a new role. My goal is to help you visualize and ultimately forge a new, more fulfilling path for yourself. One you may have never considered before.

Over the next three chapters, I am going to discuss common "but" thoughts and phrases that you may have heard before or even said to yourself. I group these into the following categories:

- Chapter 9: Money Worries
- Chapter 10: Philosophy
- Chapter 11: Other Excuses

BUT I DON'T HAVE ANY MONEY SAVED

We've already talked quite a bit about the "issue" of not having enough money, but it's worth going over one more time. Money is the biggest thing holding most of us back, whether we realize it or not.

I discussed the idea of money in Chapter 3 and how we were told in our younger days to find something you love to do each day and you will be rich. This concept was all about finding a profession that makes you happy, to do something each day where you not only will be fulfilled, but you will also earn an income to support your lifestyle. It wasn't about being financially rich but living a rich, satisfying life.

Most people realize this concept; however, as we go through our journey of life, it seems way too easy to get caught up in the concept of finding a job that pays the bills, has good health benefits, and helps save for retirement. I don't think that was the sentiment of the concept "to find something you love to do each day and you will be rich."

But for whatever reason, finding a comfortable career/job happens. Once this happens, over time, we train our brains to think that this is the best path for us. Even when we have glimpses of going after our dreams or pursuing a passion, our learned pathway takes over and says, "Stop daydreaming, silly. You need this job to pay the bills." Or fill in whatever excuse you have trained your brain to resort to.

Below, I'm restating common phrases I hear often because it's worth reiterating these mental patterns:

1. I can't leave this job that I don't like. I have a car and house payment and I have to support my children.
2. I want to travel the world [or fill in the blank with a dream you have], but I don't have any money saved yet.
3. I need to stay in my current job that I don't love because what I really want to do does not pay any money.

Money is essential for survival: health, shelter, food, safety. But if you have said any of those statements above, you have admitted that money is more important to you than personal happiness.

Don't worry, I have said all three of those statements (and many similar statements) at various points in my life. It is hard to admit this to ourselves. We are smart people. We don't want to feel that we are wrong or intentionally doing harm to ourselves or to our families in any way.

I couldn't leave my job because the money was just too good. I wanted to leave my job and travel the world, but how would I afford to pay for my travels? If I left my job, it would be zero income and 100% expenses.

I hear variations of this same thing play out with many others. It doesn't have to be travel; it could be a similar situation involving finances like, I would love to start my own business or try something new, but I can't leave my job because I have a family to support.

Many unhappy situations use money as the tether to stay. Money becomes the decision-maker. Not happiness. Not passion.

Instead, we follow this thought pattern:

1. Money is important for us to live
2. We must maintain a certain income to survive
3. We can't go backward on income
4. We fear lacking money
5. Fear suppresses creativity and imagination
6. Our dreams and passions are altered and reconsidered, even thrown away

You have been taught that money is a planning tool for your life. But for many, what this really means is that a fear of lack of money is the ultimate factor against following dreams. We fear not having money. We fear that if we try something and it doesn't work out, we won't be able to eat, live, or support our family. But come on, your happiness should matter too!

How long will you continue saying these statements until your unhappiness catches up with you? Because one day your unhappiness will be overwhelming, just like it was for me, if you don't make a change now.

Instead of just dismissing your dream, let's dive into the real fear.

What are you most afraid of related to money and pursuing an ultimate dream or passion? What are you saving for?

- **I want to be able to retire at a certain age with an amount to last me to the end.** I used to think I needed to hit a magical number of retirement dollars saved before I stopped working. I realized several things eventually: First, I can't imagine ever fully retiring and stopping something that is a big part of my life. I imagine I will be keeping my mind active managing passive income streams that I'm passionate about. Second, what if I don't live long enough to make it to retirement? Why wouldn't I want to enjoy my life now? And third, when I am earning an income in my new dream venture, why can't I continue to save money for retirement? Well, I can, but my mind continued to think I would never be able to earn as much as my corporate job. I was in my own way! I had to convince myself that I would figure it out. I kept forgetting that my goal was to create new income that has the potential to be much higher than my corporate job.

- **I want to be able to afford nice things (apartment/house in a specific neighborhood, car, clothing, etc.) to keep up with the Joneses.** Growing up in a middle-class family, I always dreamed of living in a big house in an affluent neighborhood. That was my idea of "making it." But when I made it, I realized how unhappy I truly was. Stuff didn't make me happy, and it never will make you happy. Figure out the bare minimum you need to survive and be happy. If you can't give up some things and spending habits, then make sure you are aware those are the choices you make to accommodate your lifestyle. Just be careful: when you say you don't have enough money to leave your job or pursue a passion, check to make sure you aren't spending too much on things you don't need. If you rearrange your spending, you just might be able to afford it.

- **I want to live in an urban environment, so I need the money (because cities are more expensive).** This statement is similar to the statement above, however it is slightly different because it focuses on the social benefits of your environment, not just materialistic ones. Think about the sacrifices you are willing to make while you pursue a dream or passion. I knew once I left my job that I could no longer afford to live in New York City or a larger urban environment. I had to make peace with this to pursue my passion. You may be able to get creative and remain in a more expensive urban environment by doing something like getting a roommate, moving to a cheaper part of town, keeping a job to pay your living expenses, etc. But also, keep in mind that some urban environments are not as expensive as others.

- **I want to have enough money to travel.** Two things are at play with this one: If you leave a job to travel, you won't be earning any money. In addition to earning no money, you will be spending money by traveling. It's a double whammy. But in all honesty, traveling for extended periods of time is very doable without worrying about money.

  ❑ First, traveling on a budget is a must. If you are truly passionate about travel, you must accept a different way to travel. At 40 years old, I had never stayed in a hostel before. Once I realized how economical a hostel was, I had to get out of my own way. After I began staying in hostels, I realized how much fun they were. In fact, I had more fun staying in a hostel than staying on my own. If you are traveling with someone else, you may be able to afford a different lodging situation, but as a solo traveler, you not only save a lot of money by staying at a hostel, but you meet more interesting people. I've heard many people say they could never stay in cheaper places. If that is the case, then maybe reconsider your thoughts about traveling. If you say you want to travel but have restrictions, think about the circular loop you are creating for yourself. You have a wish or passion, but you allow rules you make up to prevent you from achieving this passion. Get out of your own way.

❑ Second, there are many ways to earn income while traveling. If you own a home, consider renting it out for passive income. If you have a specific skillset you can leverage online, create a business opportunity around this to earn while traveling. Also, many people found jobs for short periods of time while traveling to help them finance their travels. I realize this is not something you may have considered, but it is important to think about what is possible. You can do anything if you get creative.

- **I need to have enough money to live (and for my family to live) while starting up a new opportunity.** This is a real concern for many who want to leave a job that produces a steady income to support themselves and perhaps a family. It is important to find ways to save now. Are there unneeded expenses you can cut? Can you change your living situation to save money? Also, if it is not possible to live 100% off savings while pursuing a new opportunity, consider getting a part-time job to earn enough to support yourself and your family while pursuing your passion.

• **What if I fail?** You have built a skillset to get to this point. You can always go back to it if you need to. However, if you never even try, then you will never know. Which of these statements is worse: Following a passion and not earning as much income as you once did—potentially having to lean on skillsets you've built over time—or never pursuing a passion and always wondering what would have happened if you tried?

I remember sitting in my Upper West Side Manhattan apartment surrounded by all of my things. My nice clothes. My luxurious lifestyle. Thinking to myself that I could never have a roommate and live in Brooklyn. I had worked hard for what I had. The idea of "going backward" seemed foolish.

Money had rewired my brain to think that if I downgraded, something would be wrong with me. It became this self-fulfilling prophecy that I had to earn more money so I could have a bigger, better place and more stuff, which was supposed to make me happier and keep me "moving forward" on the successful path.

Fear of going backward aided my decisions over time to prevent a lack of money and lifestyle status. And this fear suppressed my creativity to build sustainable happiness. I could have moved to Brooklyn or found a roommate to save money, but solving my inner turmoil was bigger than just saving money. I was on a subconscious quest for inner peace and contentment but was trapped by my views about money. I needed to get out of my own way.

I didn't go backward. Instead, I jumped. I walked away from my lifestyle and my stuff. I would have never known for sure if walking away was the correct decision until I jumped. It was the best decision of my life. It took some time, but I realized I didn't need any of those things or a large part of that lifestyle as a requirement to be successful. In fact, I was happier than I'd ever been.

The fear was all in my head. And one of the most important lessons I learned firsthand was that the journey was more valuable than the money. The journey led to adventures and paths I never knew were possible for me. Things like leading transformational retreats and starting a podcast to help others. Even writing a book like this. None of this was in my realm of "what's possible" before I left.

I had to overcome the risks and take the first step of the journey. That led to something new. And the next step led to something new. And so on and so forth.

How will you ever know if you don't do it?

Our minds have become too comfortable. We have allowed money to overrule our desire for happiness. We have officially settled.

Comfort is one of the most common problems because it is the thing our minds are trained on. We know we need to live and it costs money to live. Plus, we have become accustomed to a way of life. We have basic needs like shelter, food and health, but we also have other things in our lives on top of the basic needs. The clothing and accessories we purchase because it makes us feel good (and look good). The bottles of wine we like to consume. The home accessories we have. The nice car we decided to pay extra for each month because we have earned it. These items are all lovely. And some of you may say you can't live without. However, most of us have these things without thinking twice about it.

When we get to a point of saying we don't have any money saved AND we aren't happy with our lives, then it is time for a change. Either to save money or begin working on a path to find one that is fulfilling. This book will help motivate you to begin working on finding a more fulfilling path. In the lesson for Chapters 9-11 of the online *Companion Course,* I will walk you through how to create a plan to take these first steps.

But it is important to learn how to save.

Have you ever figured out the minimum amount of money you need to survive for a month? Only the bare essentials: Housing, food, health and car insurance, and transportation. I'm not talking about the things you don't really need. This is different for everyone, but some examples include takeout or food delivery, credit card interest, new clothing, fancy coffee, nights out drinking, unneeded substances like cigarettes, maybe even the expanded cable package, subscriptions you barely use, pricey cell phone plans, and the list goes on. If you take out those luxuries, do you suddenly have way more money? Does following your passions seem a bit more possible?

Use the monthly expense tracker provided in Chapters 9-11 of the online *Companion Course* to help you understand which expenses could be reduced or even cut to help you save and afford the things in your life that help you pursue your passions.

BUT, MY JOB PAYS TOO WELL AND HAS GREAT BENEFITS

I've met many people throughout my career who have told me, "Cory, I don't like my job, but it pays really well and has incredible benefits, so why would I ever leave?"

I find it fascinating the value that people have placed on "pays well and has great benefits." They seem to have surrendered their own happiness for money.

Being unhappy is counterintuitive to being human. I don't need to be a world-renowned scientist to know that we are wired to seek pleasure and avoid pain. Our brains are biologically wired to support happiness by releasing chemicals into our body and brain that make us feel good.

I chased money and lifestyle for about fifteen years to know that this "pays well, great benefits" thinking catches up with people. There is no way I could have endured thirty to forty years of a career surrendering my happiness. If I only have one shot on this planet and I can't take any money or benefits with me after I pass, why would I spend another day or month subjecting myself to something I don't love to do?

The "pays well, great benefits, don't like my job" pattern is most likely covering up a strong desire to find happiness, however fear has overwhelmingly taken over the decision-making process. And it has become easier and comforting to say the phrase over and over in order to not have to take any action and create extra work to find happiness again.

Acknowledging and accepting this internal fear is a logical first step. It is ok to have these feelings. However, the longer you choose not to accept these feelings and take action, the less time you have towards experiencing happiness again. The roadmap exercise in the lesson outlined in Chapters 9-11 of the online *Companion Course* will be a great tool to help you begin taking your first step towards acceptance.

When you reach the end of your life, will you be satisfied with your decision? Will you have any regrets? This is the tradeoff you must consider. I'd argue the adventures you discover through a journey of finding a more fulfilling path will be much more "rich" than spending a large portion of your life in autopilot just for the pay.

Now it's your turn:
- ❏ What are you most afraid of related to money and pursuing an ultimate dream or passion?
- ❏ What is one step you can take now to help you overcome this fear?

GET OUT OF YOUR OWN WAY: PHILOSOPHY

BUT I WILL GET TO THAT "ONE DAY"

Since I left my corporate career and created my new life-style with the ability to live and work remotely from any part of the world, I have become more attuned to what others say. I listen to their words and the timing of their words and I've noticed something very interesting.

I hear many people dreaming and wishing for a better life. However, they are unwilling to make changes now to begin living that life. It made me wonder, if people are truly unhappy, why do they stay in the unhappy situation?

I hear the phrase all the time, "You could get hit by a bus tomorrow." While people say that to prove a point, I don't think people truly believe it could happen to them. Most people think they will live forever. However, we never know when we will take our last breath.

It baffles me when I see people making decisions that create unhappiness, living their lives unfulfilled, or thinking they will "one day" do something they have always dreamed of doing.

I hear people wanting, wishing, dreaming, hoping after "one day." What they are really saying is, "I can't do it now because I am too afraid of doing it."

This is exactly why most people won't live their best life: because it is too uncomfortable and scary to think about moving away from the "comfort" they have created in their mind. This is why individuals in an abusive relationship are not able to just walk away. It's not as simple as that. I know all too well what it is like to feel like you have no way out. How it's just easier to stay and be abused than to take the very uncomfortable steps to get out of the situation.

Make a list of five to ten things to which you have said, "I will do that one day." The list could include a bucket list travel destination or a job or career you have wanted to pursue or learning something new. Then, pick one of these items and make a plan to accomplish this over the next three to six months. No more "one day." Do it now!

BUT THIS ISN'T FOR ME

We do funny things when life becomes too difficult or too uncomfortable. Based on previous patterning, our minds create stories for us to grab on to. We tell ourselves believable statements that will (temporarily) help us feel better about a situation.

One of the big stories our minds tend to create is to tell ourselves that a big life change is not something we want. When it becomes too hard for our brains to think of all the necessary steps, we begin to say that this was something we didn't really want anyway.

Our gut is screaming loudly for us to make a bold move, but it's easier to say "this just isn't for me."

"This isn't for me" cuts your mind off from trying new experiences. It's a non-starter. You are saying "I may fail, therefore, I don't even have to try."

When something is too hard, we convince ourselves that the difficult path is not for us. We don't want to manage uncertainty in our minds. We don't want to create extra work for ourselves and it's easier to render the extra work unnecessary. It is easier to surrender toward the path we already know.

Next time you catch yourself saying "this isn't for me," ask yourself: Is this something my gut is telling me to do but I am saying no because I'm afraid of failing or because it is too overwhelming to think about? If yes, then create a plan to break apart the tasks and take one step at a time. Try not to cut yourself off from trying something new, because this is where growth and success lives.

BUT MY JOB DOESN'T MAKE MY LIFE COMPLETE; IT IS ONLY ONE PART OF IT

Have you ever wondered how you spend your waking hours? If you sleep the recommended 8 hours each night, that means you are only awake about 16 hours. If you work 8 hours each day, spend 30 minutes preparing yourself to go to work and spend 30 to 60 minutes commuting, then you are spending between 9 and 10 hours doing something related to your job. That is about 55-60% of your waking hours.

If you say your job is only part of your life, this is a true statement. But it is a very large part of your life. In fact, if you counted up everything else that makes up your life, like exercise, eating, family time, etc., you will find your job probably takes up the largest slice of the pie. If this is your excuse, you are doing something that takes up over half of your waking hours and is not making you happy.

Your mind is trying keep you comfortable. But your mind isn't helping you be happy.

Calculate how much time each week you spend on every part of your life: work, sleep, family, personal, fitness, etc. Make sure you include the full 24 hours of each day and all seven days of the week—all 168 hours, including your days off. Make sure you use a typical week of your life and not a week of vacation or a week that includes a holiday. To help you make the calculation, download the spreadsheet template in the Chapters 9-11 Resources section of the free online *Companion Course.* What are you spending most of your week doing? How would you like to be spending your time?

BUT MY UNHAPPY SITUATION
IS ONLY TEMPORARY

Another common trap our minds love to create is telling ourselves that this current situation is only temporary.

When you tell yourself this, your mind can easily be convinced that you can be unhappy for just a bit longer when at some point in the future (in my case, two years) you will be in the clear and on a path toward happiness.

I tried this for at least six years at PepsiCo. I would tell myself that even though I'm unhappy in my current role, I will soon be eligible for a promotion and looking for a new role within the company in a year or two.

Then guess what? Once I had this new role, it provided a challenge during the first several months while I learned something new. But after this newness wore off, the same gut feeling popped up. I'm unhappy, but since I would be looking at a new role again in eighteen months, I suffered through it.

Eighteen months later, I had a new role. Three months later, I was saying the exact same thing again. The cycle continued.

We do this in many situations in our lives, including in relationships. "Oh, my situation is only temporary. It will get better at some point in the future." Are we that naive to think that our situation will get better if we are not taking steps toward resolving the deeper issues that lurk within?

My underlying issue was my unhappiness in the corporate world. I continued telling myself that my situation was temporary and that things will get better in the future.

How long must we continue through the same pattern before we stop the cycle from repeating? We must address the deep, underlying issues.

It is important to pay attention to these potentially harmful patterns in our lives. Go back to Chapter 5: "Lesson 2 - Write Your 2-Column Resume" in the online *Companion Course* and review your responses. Use this exercise to discover your feelings during each moment of your career. And see if you notice spans of time you tried to convince yourself that your moment of unhappiness was only temporary. Was it truly temporary, or is there a pattern you have discovered?

BUT I DON'T KNOW WHAT I WANT

I've heard this frequently. "I'm unhappy, but I don't know what I want to do." It is the all too common circumstance of feeling stuck in a situation that we don't know how to get out of. We know we aren't happy, yet our minds are unable to come up with a solution.

My father would consistently use this phrase. He liked his job as an electrician at times, but he knew there was something more fulfilling he could be doing. Each time I asked what that was, he would respond, "I don't know what I want to do."

Think about how he must have felt trapped in his situation every day. He knew he had other passions, yet he also knew his job paid the bills. He made a surrender, of sorts.

Saying, "I don't know what I want to do" over and over is 100% procrastination. We are avoiding taking a hard look at ourselves in the mirror and making decisions.

When we think of a situation in our lives we need to change, we often are unable to decide at the immediate point in time. Our minds initially think about the problem, and then we pause. We go about our daily lives without necessarily focusing on the problem. However, during this period, our minds subconsciously think about the situation. Sometimes we may come up with the solution without actively thinking about it.

Have you ever been sleeping soundly and suddenly you wake up with an idea to solve a situation that has been lingering? This is our subconscious mind at work.

Not all procrastination is bad. However, chronic procrastination is deadly. It is when we constantly avoid a complex issue because it is too overwhelming. When it comes to figuring out happiness in our lives and for our future, we become stumped. This situation is multi-faceted, with so many unknowns it is often easier for us to avoid the problem altogether.

But how long can we avoid answering this question? Six months, a year, three years, five years, 10 years, 40 years? While procrastinating for a while can be okay, even productive, procrastinating forever creates a slew of side effects, many of which will blunt our own happiness and progress in life.

My father was never able to pursue his passions full time. He could have created a woodworking business or a business flipping homes or even his own body shop. He was talented in many ways. He was able to spend some time on those passions in the evenings and the weekends, but he surrendered to the fact he would "one day" work on those passions. Yet he never did.

After procrastination comes regret. Wishing you would have done something years ago. Saying things like, "If I would have just done this, then…" We are unable to get those years back. We can't undo our actions and make a different choice or an actual decision instead of procrastinating.

It's time you begin to figure it out. First, stop saying you don't know what you want to do. Each time you say that, your brain continues to be strengthened with the belief that you won't figure it out. It will become a life-long belief.

Second, build a roadmap to figure out what you want to do right now. Like I discussed earlier, I think one of the common misconceptions about a career is that you must pick one that you will have forever. It is difficult to find something we want to do forever. Your path can take you to many different types of careers. Find one that feels good to you right now. And then, if you ever outgrow this career, find a new one that fits at that point in time.

BUT I'M TOO OLD TO DO THAT

It's easy for you, you are young and have time to do that.

I only have ten years before I retire. I'm stuck doing this.

I've invested 30 years into this. I can't just leave now.

I'm too old to do that.

The age-old "old age" excuse. Yes, it is an excuse. It is another way for our mind to stay comfortable. To just "grin and bear it." To continue rationalizing our unhappiness and calm our guts down.

Age is just a number. It really is.

When we were younger, our decision-making and thought patterns were all freewheeling. We knew we could make a decision, and if it didn't pan out, we had time to remedy the situation. For example, if we took a job right out of college, it didn't matter so much if the job sucked. We knew we just wanted a first job and it would be a stepping stone to another, better job. We were willing to take on more risk when it came to our careers.

Even in relationships, we knew early in our dating lives that if the first date flopped, we had many opportunities and time to find another date. First-date fails and relationships in our twenties and even early thirties didn't feel that bad because we knew we still had runway for something better in the future.

However, a funny thing begins to occur as we age. With each time around the sun, it feels like our birthday arrives one day earlier every year. Over time, it feels like our days move faster and faster. Each year we are different people, with a different body and a different future. And because of this, our decisions begin to reflect this different future as we realize we won't be around forever.

I like to imagine a runway. During our younger days, the runway was extremely long. It didn't matter if we messed up, because if we were trying to take off, we didn't have to go as fast to succeed. We had plenty of time to figure it out.

As we move down the runway and veer around obstacles, the runway becomes shorter. Our thinking becomes shorter and shorter and shorter as a result.

Let's imagine you have had the same career for 30 years. You received an undergraduate degree and you have remained in the same field since you graduated. This field is okay, but your passion lies outside of this career.

You have spent your entire adult life in this field. You worked with a financial advisor, who told you that in 10 years you'd be able to end your career and live the rest of your years comfortably. Your entire mindset is focused on: "I just have to make it ten more years. I have worked hard to get this far, so I can get to the end."

Everything you have subconsciously trained your brain to do is working. You have trained your brain that there is one path: work, earn, retire. You have convinced yourself that retirement is the only option and have trained your brain to think you will be able to be happy once you reach that point. You and your financial advisor have laid out a roadmap. You know exactly when you will be set to retire. Then you will finally be free.

Plus, on top of all of this, your brain reminds you that you are in the prime earning years of your career. Now is not the time to give any of that up. You have surrendered and are forging ahead because that is the best option for the next ten years (which, by the way, is a large percentage of your lifespan).

Each of these reminders has comforted your brain. The planning has eliminated risk, for the most part. Of course there are worldly events that could disrupt this plan, like a financial crisis or a global pandemic like covid-19, but for the most part, your mind is comforted knowing you can eventually sail into the sunset.

Your thinking has been limited. You have wired your brain over the past 30 years of your career to think that your 10-year plan to stay in your unhappy job is the best option. It becomes difficult to remember important facts like the bullet points below that could help you rewire your brain toward a new path (by jumping) without wasting 10 years of potential happiness:

- You have saved for most of your career and have built up savings. If you really wanted to leave your career to pursue something new, you would have a way to do this.
- Maybe you even own property that has value or have other types of investments. While you may have a mortgage payment, you could continue to make payments or you have options to adjust your living situation.
- Retirement isn't what it used to be where we just sit around in a warm climate. Most of us want to be active in retirement, so we pursue our passions. Will you be bored in retirement? If you are going to pursue your hobbies and passions in retirement, why wouldn't you begin now?

Our brains are wired to adapt to the shortening of the runway. But what is the end of the runway? Is it your retirement date? Is it the end of your life? The date is arbitrary. Understanding this principle of a shortened runway helps us plan, but what ends up happening is this principle becomes a limit we have created for our lives. It limits our ability to think beyond this "plan." It narrows our thinking into the path we have been trained to follow.

As the runway becomes shorter, these limits become tighter. We take fewer risks to protect ourselves.

What would you have to believe to take your risk? Do you need specific guarantees? Are those guarantees influenced by what you've been trained to think? What is possible in your life if you did take that risk?

Anything is possible, but you must shift your thinking first. You must realize that the runway is not real. We tend to forget about the upside associated with taking the risk. We fail to consider the journey and instead only focus on the destination, when the journey will lead to much greater happiness and fulfillment than whatever awaits us when we get there.

Consider volunteering your time doing something you love to do. Volunteering is a great gateway leading to other opportunities within organizations you are passionate about.

Consider teaching yourself something new related to your passion. Technology has made it incredibly easy to learn new skills and even trades online. Use it to your advantage. If you don't know technology that well, take the time to learn it.

Reread the following statements we discussed in this chapter out loud:

- I will get to that one day...
- This isn't for me...
- My job is only part of my life...
- My situation is only temporary...
- I don't know what I want...
- I'm too old for that...

You can hear a story, complete with characters, setting, plot, and conflict, in these statements. When life decisions become complex, we often create these stories for our minds to latch onto as a coping mechanism.

These stories are replayed in our minds to help steer us toward safety, and if we don't pay attention, they eventually become our operating manuals, with logical information left out. Pay attention to the stories that you have always told yourself. Ask yourself what value is this story adding to your ultimate purpose and happiness. If it is no longer serving you, it probably is time to get out of your own way and rewrite your story.

Now it's your turn:
- ❑ What life situation do you habitually procrastinate, but know in your gut that you need to resolve?
- ❑ What is one step you can take today or this week to begin working towards resolving this life situation?
- ❑ What story do you replay over and over in your mind to avoid a complex situation?

GET OUT OF
YOUR OWN WAY:
OTHER EXCUSES

BUT I AM MARRIED AND HAVE A FAMILY TO SUPPORT

Family and children are a huge priority in many people's lives. However, our lives are multi-faceted, and people can use family and children as an excuse to avoid thinking about their own happiness.

Does the statement "I can't begin a new career because I have to support my family" also mean you must surrender your happiness of pursuing a dream or passion? Maybe raising your children is your passion, which is incredible. Then you are living that passion. However, I have met many parents who struggle raising their children and look for something more fulfilling in their careers.

We often feel guilty when we think about prioritizing our own happiness over a responsibility of raising a family or building a relationship with someone. Selflessness is certainly an admirable quality; however, finding balance is more important than being pushed to the edge.

When we focus most of our time and energy on our family and relationships, we risk diminishing our own well-being. When our well-being and happiness levels decrease, this puts the focus we spend on our family and our relationships at risk.

Stop using family as a distraction to avoid discovering your own happiness. Find out what you want as an individual, and *then* figure out how to fit this in with your family role. Remember, if you are not happy, then you can have a negative impact on the rest of your family.

If you are married/in a relationship, talk about your career-based unhappiness with your partner and discuss your desire to quit with them. Set a day and add time on your calendar now so you won't forget.

BUT I HAVE A HEALTH CONDITION

Staying healthy is a part of our everyday lives. I've always said my "body is my temple." I make sure I respect my body and give it the care that it needs. We need a healthy mind and body to carry our soul through this crazy journey of life.

However, I know for many, health can be a sensitive topic. Our bodies and minds are all genetically built different and our lifestyles vary dramatically. As a result of these differences, our minds and bodies certainly are not equal.

Health conditions exist and can alter our lives. Sometimes they impact our ability to perform specific tasks. I bring up this topic because I have heard individuals use their own health or a specific condition as a barrier to moving forward in life.

This book is about overcoming adversity and career struggle. While many of us don't choose an adverse health condition, we can choose how to react to and overcome them. Not only physically, but also mentally. I often hear others use their health condition as a way to limit themselves. Just as the other excuses listed above, a health condition can be used to calm the mind and keep it in a comfortable place. If your health is holding you back because of the money (maybe a health condition is so expensive that it is impossible to quit your job), not the motivation, reread Chapter 9 - Get Out Of Your Own Way: Money.

Think about the stories we often hear of amputees, people who are blind, those battling cancer, and many others in difficult physical or health situations who have run marathons, competed in triathlons, climbed Mount Everest, or conquered other feats. These individuals have been pushed up against adversity, yet have seemed to overcome these limitations to accomplish a goal.

On a recent retreat I led for the transformational travel company I founded, one of the adventures we experienced was climbing a mountain in the heart of Bali. We began climbing in the pre-dawn hours to reach the summit before the sun peaked over the ocean's horizon in the distance.

Laura, a 62-year-old woman who had been battling Stage IV breast cancer, received the go-ahead from her oncologist to attend this life-changing retreat. It could very well be one of the last trips of her life.

During the weeks leading up to the trip, Laura trained for the mountain hike by climbing steep inclines in her community during her walk. She hadn't exercised in years because the treatments she had endured through many types of health setbacks made her weak. One year prior to the trip, she didn't even have the energy to get out of bed for months at a time. However, she had fought and fought and fought. With her health improving, she was more determined than ever to go on this retreat but most importantly conquer the mountain.

Laura popped her chemo pill before making her way up the steep mountain in Crocs in the middle of Bali, determined to conquer. And she did.

She had nothing to lose. At times, Laura slid down the loose gravel as she tried to advance up the mountain. Not only was she out of breath from climbing 1,200 meters, but the elevation impact made the oxygen levels even lighter. Her physical fitness was subpar and her equipment amateur, yet she did it.

Climbing that mountain is the metaphor of life. We started in the middle of the night with a gradual incline. We got used to hiking in the jungle. Then the incline steepened. The obstacles became more impactful. We fell down at times and had many setbacks. But we got back up. We took breaks to catch our breath. And as the incline seemed too steep to climb, we helped each other conquer the feat. We encouraged each other to keep going. Our mental chatter told us many times that we should just stop, yet we pushed onward to accomplish the goal.

We must realize that anything is possible in life. Even when our health seems to set us back, we must remember to toughen our minds. We are able to do anything we want to do.

You can climb your own mountain. Having a pre-existing health condition certainly is challenging and comes with obstacles. But if Laura can climb the mountain after taking a chemo pill, a pill that often makes you nauseous and can lower your energy levels, then you can also go after what you want to do.

It's easy for us to surrender to a health condition, including mental conditions like anxiety or moments of depression. These situations aren't ideal. These conditions exist. And these conditions—through the storyline we create—often train our brains to stagnate, to remain as we are. And as a result, the health condition holds us in place and eventually prevents us from thinking of what else is possible.

Over time, we lean on these conditions and use them to rationalize why we haven't been able to go after what we really want in life.

Health conditions impact our physical state; however, the impact to the mental state can often be overlooked. Our minds are the strongest and most important tool that we have.

Leaving an unhappy job because of a health situation may not be an option for some. If you are unable to leave your current position because of your health, ask yourself: Is it because of the (lack of) motivation or is it because of the money/health benefits? If it is due to the latter, then ask yourself how can you creatively follow your passion while receiving the health benefits you require. Do other positions exist within your organization that would be more fulfilling? Are you able to make slight adjustments to your current position that would improve your happiness? Maybe certain work-life balance benefits or a flexible work schedule? This is your moment to be creative and think about what is possible for you.

If your decision to stay is because of a lack of motivation, then consider trying something new that may be slightly outside of your comfort zone. It doesn't have to be a new career, but try something different than your normal daily routine. Maybe it is related to your career or maybe it is related to your personal life. It could be as simple as walking around the block, or it could be more complex, like climbing a mountain.

Go back and reread the lessons of Part 2: How to Jump. Listen to your gut. Take time to think. Use this moment in time, reading this book, to begin making small adjustments. Your "Jump" is trying one new thing you have never done before. And then try another.

BUT I'M ALL PLANNING AND NOT DOING

So you have an idea and you begin planning. You write down your plan and create action steps to reach your goal. You continue to build on these action steps and before you know it, you have spent hours on planning but have not done anything. You learn that taking the first action step is super hard to do, so you procrastinate.

Eventually, you take some action steps, but you find that you are back in planning mode. In fact, you spend all your time planning and little time doing. Maybe you have done something like accumulate a list of books to read, but you haven't been able to start with the first book. Or you dove deep into personal development lessons, webinars, and online courses, but never took their suggested steps toward doing anything.

I am an expert at this. I've learned that I love to plan and I am very good at it. However, I often fail to launch. I just love the planning aspect. I've found the steps needed to accomplish my goal can be overwhelming and often require a skill that I don't have. So then I create a plan to either obtain this skill or find someone else who can help me with this skill.

We often have dreams and passions that we think will be incredible; however, the steps to get there are overwhelming. For many of us, they require something we don't know how to do yet.

How do we problem-solve to get ourselves moving forward again? I find that this is where many people break down. A few years prior to writing this book, I had this brief idea to sell wallets. I was no expert designing wallets, nor did I know anything about manufacturing, supply chain and distribution. I planned and planned and planned. I had a solid plan. But this plan was never executed because I lacked the energy and passion to learn what I needed to get the business off the ground.

If you are someone who loves to plan, begin doing. Create a list of steps to take, but then begin working on the first one, and the first one only. It is impossible to multitask things that require critical and creative thinking. Prioritize your list and only complete the first task before moving on to the next one. Also, make sure you focus on one project at a time. I suggest reading the book *The ONE Thing: The Surprisingly Simple Truth Behind Extraordinary Results* by Gary Keller and Jay Papsan to help nail down this concept.

Now it's your turn:
- ❑ Which statement throughout Chapters 9-11 do you tell yourself most often?
- ❑ Are there other statements or excuses you use to keep your mind comfortable?
- ❑ What are ways that you can reverse the statement to ask, "what is possible?"

ONLINE EXERCISE

Go to "Chapters 9-11 - Get Out Of Your Own Way" of

the *Jump Without A Parachute Companion Course* at

JUMPWITHOUTAPARACHUTE.COM/COURSE

and get ready to create your roadmap to help

you jump and overcome your excuses.

JUMP

September 25, 2017, was the day I walked into the PepsiCo World Headquarters to ask for my leave of absence. I will always remember it as the day I threw the parachute off to the side and jumped without it. I finally listened to my gut and took the leap.

And I've been on the greatest personal transformation of my life ever since that day.

After I learned everything I shared with you in this book, I succeeded in living the life of my dreams. I no longer dread going to sleep on Sunday evening knowing what lies ahead on Monday morning. I no longer stare out the window thinking about the life I could be living, because I'm living how I want to live. I no longer worry about not knowing what I want to do. I no longer wonder what company I will work for next when I become unhappy in my job.

I've finally realized that other career paths exist. I am no longer tied to an enticing corporate path filled with fancy buzzwords, perks, and award structures used as bread crumbs along a corporate path designed to keep my unhappy mind occupied, locking me into years of meaningless service. How empty does that sound?

Jumping without a parachute has allowed me to experience life in a new and exciting way. I have life flexibilities that were not afforded while tied to a corporate job. I'm now able to live anywhere. I'm able to work anywhere in the world at any time. The idea of a nine-to-five workweek no longer applies. I've been able to chase the sun and avoid cold winters. I've been able to watch my niece's and nephew's sporting events in the summertime. I'm able to travel and see the world at my own pace.

In addition to this newfound life flexibility, I've learned invaluable skills that I would have never fully obtained in the rat race. I'm building my own personal brand and ecosystem of inspiration by creating new businesses and products from scratch. I'm living my higher purpose each moment and watching people have their own breakthrough moments in life as a result of the content and products I've created.

I've written and published a bestselling book, I've created a successful and life-changing travel company, I've launched an inspirational podcast, I've coached individuals and small business owners to reach ultimate success, and I'm now sharing the lessons I've learned along this journey with you.

This book has provided you with a roadmap to help you take the leap and jump toward success. You know how to listen to your gut. You know how to take time to think. You know that failing is important to success. You know how to forget about your holdups. You have learned many important tools that will help you succeed. You now have what you need to jump.

Remember those moments at home where you dread going into work? Those moments at work where you wish you weren't there? Those moments where you daydream of something more fulfilling? Dreaming of not being tied down to your current situation?

Now, after reading this book, you have a brand-new lens. You have come so far. Ultimately, you have built the confidence to begin living the life of your choice. I can't wait to watch what happens next for you.

Now that you are prepared, get ready to focus on happiness, not money. Find out how you can quit, and do it. Take those risks.

When will be your September 25th? When will be that day you remember for the rest of your life as the beginning of fulfillment and happiness? The day you said 'YES' to YOU! Why not make that day today?

Forget the parachute. Just jump.

ONLINE EXERCISE

Go to "Chapter 12 - Jump" of the

Jump Without A Parachute Companion Course at

JUMPWITHOUTAPARACHUTE.COM/COURSE

and complete the course to receive

your completion certificate.

Thank you for buying this book!

I would appreciate your feedback on what chapters helped you most, and what you would like to see in future books.

If you enjoyed this book and found it helpful, please leave a REVIEW on Amazon.

If this book inspired you to jump and you would like to share your personal jump story, please visit www.jumpwithoutaparachute.com

Visit my personal page at www.corycalvin.com, where you can sign up for email updates about my upcoming books and transformational businesses.

Connect with me directly by email:
cory@corycalvin.com

Thank you!

ACKNOWLEDGMENTS

They say it takes a village to raise a child, and in many ways writing a book like this takes a village. This book is the culmination of countless hours of work all dedicated to helping others make the brave decision to take a big leap. And I am humbled by the number of people who have generously supported me personally on this journey, and who have supported this book. It would be impossible to thank everyone who had an impact, but there are a few people who deserve specific mention, because without them, this book would not have been possible.

My family is at the top of that list, starting with my mother, Melanie. While she is not physically among us anymore, her presence is around me every day. She taught me to be brave, to believe in myself and to shoot for my passions and dreams. I wouldn't be the person I am today without her. Mom, I love you to the moon and back.

My sister, Abby Calvin, my niece, Breanna Richmond, and my nephew, Brandon Buehrer, for your unconditional love and support of my work and life.

My best friend Amanda Koluch has been my rock throughout my life post-college. Your love and support in every area of my life has been so special to me and I am thankful for you every day. And to Amanda's mom, Cyndi Alte, thank you for your love and support and for being such a special person in my life.

A special thank you goes to my spiritual and life mentor, Debi Havens. You are an incredible and positive force in my life who has helped me unlock my life in so many ways. Thank you for being my second mom.

Thank you to my army of early readers who provided valuable feedback to make this body of work even stronger. Steve Toppercov, Alexander Gonzalez, Holly Sprow, Vicky Moore, Heidi Stark, Jeneva Augello, Bruce Weinkauf, Kerry Harding, and Michael Whisler.

Thank you to all members of my book tribe for your feedback along the way on topics, chapters, stories and book cover designs.

Thank you to Camille Benitah, the Frenchwoman who welcomed me to her table at the Yoga Barn in Ubud, Bali, Indonesia, who inspired me to leave my corporate life and learn that home is always within me. And that I can go back home at any time.

Qat Wanders and her team at Wandering Words Media, thank you for the hours to help develop and edit my book. Rochelle Deans for your incredible clean-up work and editing. 100 Covers, especially Micah Marquez, for coordinating such a stand out cover design for this book. Formatted Books for the unique book layout. Rachel Reclam for the unique worksheet templates and designs in the online *Companion Course*.

ABOUT THE AUTHOR

Cory Calvin grew up in rural Ohio. A 2001 graduate of Ball State University, Cory began his career in New York City on Wall Street and went on to receive his MBA from the University of Florida. After 16 years as a corporate finance and strategy executive, Cory left the 9-to-5 world behind and created his personal brand and ecosystem of transformational offerings from scratch, all while traveling the world. Cory leads transformational global retreats and trips with his company Pivot Trip and hosts his inspirational podcast "The Cory Calvin Podcast." His first book, *I Almost Became Me: A Memoir* became an Amazon Bestseller in May 2019 and he seeks to inspire one million people over the next 10 years.

Made in USA - Kendallville, IN
1176504_9781733930635
10.07.2020 0824